READING FUNDAMENTALS

by Susan Schader Lee

GRADE

2

New York

New York

An Imprint of Sterling Publishing
1166 Avenue of the Americas
New York, NY 10036

ISBN 978-1-4114-7200-6

Distributed in Canada by Sterling Publishing
c/o Canadian Manda Group, 664 Annette Street
Toronto, Ontario, Canada M6S 2C8
Distributed in the United Kingdom by GMC Distribution Services
Castle Place, 166 High Street, Lewes, East Sussex, England BN7 1XU
Distributed in Australia by Capricorn Link (Australia) Pty. Ltd.
P.O. Box 704, Windsor, NSW 2756, Australia

For information about custom editions, special sales, and premium and
corporate purchases, please contact Sterling Special Sales at 800-805-
5489 or specialsales@sterlingpublishing.com.

Manufactured in Canada
Lot #:
2 4 6 8 10 9 7 5 3
02/16

www.flashkids.com

Dear Parent,

Being able to read and understand nonfiction texts is an essential skill that not only ensures success in the classroom, but also in college and beyond. Why is nonfiction reading important? For one thing, close reading of nonfiction texts helps build critical-thinking skills. Another reason nonfiction reading is important is that it builds your child's background knowledge. That means your child will already have a wealth of knowledge about various subjects to build on as he or she progresses in school. You can feel good knowing you'll be laying the foundation for future success by ensuring that your child develops the necessary skills that nonfiction reading comprehension provides.

The activities in this workbook are meant for your child to be able to do on his or her own. However, you can assist your child with difficult words, ideas, and questions. Reading comprehension skills take time to develop, so patience is important. After your child has completed each activity, you can go over the answers together using the answer key provided in the back of this workbook. Provide encouragement and a sense of accomplishment to your child as you go along!

Extending reading comprehension beyond this workbook is beneficial and provides your child with the opportunity to see why this skill is so essential. You might read a newspaper article together and then discuss the main ideas, or head to the library to find a book on your child's favorite subject. Remember, reading is fun. It opens the door to imagination!

Life Cycle of a Butterfly

Have you ever seen a baby butterfly? If you have seen a caterpillar, then you have! Butterflies start their lives as worm-like caterpillars. This is called the larva stage.

Butterflies lay eggs on plants. Some types of butterflies lay only one egg at a time. Other types lay up to a few hundred at a time! Caterpillars hatch from the eggs. They are very tiny at first. The main job for caterpillars is to eat a lot and grow. They eat the leaves of the plant where they hatched.

Caterpillars then begin the pupa stage. They form a cocoon around themselves. Some types of caterpillars stay in their cocoons for only a few days. Other types stay inside for many months. But all of them go through an amazing change! This change is called a metamorphosis.

After the metamorphosis is done, they come out of their cocoons. But they are no longer worm-like babies! They are adult butterflies. They have beautiful wings. Adult butterflies do not live very long. Most of them live only two to four weeks. None of them live more than one year. So they start laying eggs right away. The cycle starts again!

Read each sentence. Circle *true* or *false*.

1. Butterflies lay eggs on plants.	true	false
2. Caterpillars form cocoons around themselves.	true	false
3. Adult butterflies live for a long time.	true	false
4. Caterpillars start their lives as butterflies.	true	false

A Race to the Moon

Neil Armstrong was a famous astronaut. He was the first person to walk on the moon!

When the 1960s started, no person had ever been to outer space. The United States wanted to put the first person in space. So did another country called Russia. The United States and Russia were in a race! Russia won the race. In 1961, a Russian man flew a spacecraft around Earth.

But the race was not over! The United States kept trying. Just three weeks later, the first American flew into space. Then the United States announced a new goal. It wanted to put the first person on the moon! The United States spent many years testing spacecraft. It trained astronauts. Finally, the Apollo 11 spacecraft was ready. So were the astronauts. Neil Armstrong was the commander of the spacecraft.

In July 1969, the Apollo 11 spacecraft landed on the moon! It took four days to get there. Neil Armstrong was the first person to walk on the moon. His footprints are still there today!

Finish each sentence.

1. When the 1960s started, no one had yet been to _____ .

2. The United States and _____ were in a race to outer space.

3. _____ was the commander of the Apollo 11 spacecraft.

4. Neil Armstrong's _____ are still on the moon.

The Cotton Gin

Did you know that cotton grows from a plant? Well, it does! That means cotton has seeds in it. Farmers need to take out the seeds before they can sell the cotton. But how?

In India, cotton farmers used a special machine to pick out seeds. It was called a cotton churka. In the 1600s, farmers started growing cotton in North America. First the farmers used the cotton churka. But the churka only worked for some kinds of cotton. For other kinds, people had to pick out the seeds by hand. This took a long time! Farmers wanted to sell more cotton. They needed a faster way to pick out the seeds.

Eli Whitney was an American inventor. In 1793, he invented a new machine called the cotton gin. The cotton gin was similar to the churka. But it worked on all kinds of cotton plants. Farmers started using the new cotton gin. Now they could sell more cotton! Clothing made from cotton became very popular.

Read each question. Circle the right answer.

1. Where does cotton come from?

   a) a plant   b) a churka   c) clothing

2. What does cotton have in it?   a) water   b) seeds   c) stems

3. What does a churka do?

   a) grow cotton   b) sell cotton   c) pick out cotton seeds

4. Who invented the cotton gin?

   a) farmers   b) Eli Whitney   c) Native Americans

Pangea

There are seven continents on Earth. That is, there are seven large landmasses. They are Africa, Antarctica, Asia, Australia, Europe, North America, and South America. But this was not always the case!

The seven continents used to be one big supercontinent. It was called Pangea. Pangea lasted for millions of years. The land started to break apart more than 200 million years ago. The separate landmasses moved away from each other. This took a very long time. Now there is lots of ocean water between the continents.

How do we know about Pangea? Scientists found clues from fossils. Old fossils show similar plants and animals on different continents. How could plants and animals be the same on opposite sides of the world? It is because the continents used to be connected!

Find a map of the world. Look at the seven continents. Can you see how they once fit together like a puzzle?

Read each sentence. Circle *true* or *false*.

1. Today there are seven continents on Earth.	true	false
2. Pangea existed just a few years ago.	true	false
3. Fossils gave scientists clues about Pangea.	true	false
4. Most continents are still connected.	true	false

Create a Terrarium!

An ecosystem is a community of plants or animals and their environment. You can build a mini-ecosystem to observe. Create a plant terrarium!

Find a large glass jar. It is best if the opening is wide. This makes it easier to put plants inside. Place a layer of small stones at the bottom of the jar. The stones allow extra water to drain. Add a layer of charcoal. The charcoal filters the water. Then add potting soil. The soil layer should be thicker than the stones and charcoal.

Now it is time to choose your plants! Be sure to choose plants that need the same kind of environment. You could use all cacti. They need very little water. Or you could use ferns and mosses. These plants need lots of water. Be sure to leave space between the plants. They need room to breathe and grow!

Put your terrarium in a bright area. But make sure it is not in the direct sun! If your terrarium gets too hot, the plants can die. Add some water. After the first time, you will not need to water the plants very much. Your mini-ecosystem has everything it needs to thrive!

Answer the questions below.

1. What kind of container should you use for your terrarium?

_____

2. What is the job of the stones in your terrarium?

_____

3. What is the job of the charcoal in your terrarium?

_____

4. Can you mix any types of plants together in your terrarium?

_____

Independence Day

The Fourth of July is a popular holiday in the United States. It is also called Independence Day. People have parties and parades. They celebrate with fireworks. Do you know what they are celebrating?

In the 1700s, there were thirteen British colonies on American land. This meant that England controlled the colonies. The thirteen colonies rebelled. They wanted to be free from British rule.

They fought against Britain in the Revolutionary War. On July 4, 1776, the colonies signed the Declaration of Independence. It said that the colonies were separate from Britain.

Americans have celebrated Independence Day ever since. They dress in the colors of the American flag: red, white, and blue. They shoot off fireworks. In the colonies, people fired guns to celebrate. Watching controlled fireworks is safer. Americans have Fourth of July parties to celebrate America's birthday. Happy birthday, America!

Finish each sentence.

1. The Fourth of July is also called _____ .

2. Thirteen colonies fought _____ in the Revolutionary War.

3. The colonies were fighting for _____ from British rule.

4. Now, we shoot off _____ to celebrate the Fourth of July.

Your Five Senses

People have five senses. They are sight, touch, hearing, smell, and taste. We use these senses to experience the world.

We use our eyes for sight. We rely on sight to know where we are. We rely on sight to know who is near. We rely on sight to know what food is on our plates. We use our sense of sight a lot! With an adult's help, try blindfolding yourself. Can you move through your bedroom without bumping into things? Can you know who is talking to you? Can you know what food you are eating?

The answers to those questions are probably yes! This is because we rarely use just one sense at a time. We use our senses together to gather information. Your sense of touch can help you move through your room. Your hands feel what furniture might be in your way. Your sense of hearing can help you know who is talking. Your ears hear their voices. Your senses of smell and taste help you know what food you are eating. Your nose smells the food. And your tongue tastes it. It is hard to say which sense we use the most!

Draw a line to match the words with the pictures.

touch   taste   sight   hearing   smell

It's a Twister!

Tornadoes are severe windstorms. Sometimes they are called twisters. This is because the storms twist and whirl. Tornadoes look like spinning tubes of wind. Sometimes they look like funnels. Tornado winds are very powerful. They can destroy anything in their paths. They can rip houses to shreds. They can uproot trees. They can throw cars far away. Tornadoes are very dangerous storms!

Tornadoes form from thunderstorms. They stretch from a storm cloud down to the ground. The spinning air travels very fast. Tornadoes do a lot of damage while they travel. But they are over quickly! Most tornadoes die out after just a few miles.

Most tornadoes in the United States happen in the Great Plains. Many take place in an area called Tornado Alley. The main states that make up Tornado Alley include Texas, Oklahoma, Kansas, and Nebraska. Florida has a lot of tornadoes too.

It is a good idea to stay away from windows during a tornado. The best place to be is underground. Basements are great places to hide from the storm!

Read each question. Circle the right answer.

1. Why are tornadoes called twisters?   a) Because they can destroy houses.
   b) Because they are powerful.   c) Because their winds twist and whirl.

2. For how long do tornadoes last?   a) days   b) minutes   c) hours

3. Which states are in Tornado Alley?
   a) Texas, Florida, and Oklahoma   b) Kansas, Nebraska, and Florida
   c) Oklahoma, Kansas, and Nebraska

4. Where is the safest place to be during a tornado?
   a) underground   b) in a car   c) next to the window

The Pony Express

Mail used to travel very slowly across the United States. Some of it traveled by stagecoaches or covered wagons. But the United States kept expanding west. People needed a faster way to send mail!

In 1860, some men started the Pony Express. The Pony Express was a system to send mail by horseback. Riders carried mail on horseback between Missouri and California. They stopped at lots of stations along the way. At each station, they switched to a new horse. This way, the horses could rest. It took about ten days to travel the whole route. This was much faster than before!

There were some problems with the Pony Express. It was dangerous for the riders and horses! They rode in bad weather. They rode over rough terrain. Also, the company that started the Pony Express lost a lot of money.

The Pony Express only lasted for a year and a half. Then the transcontinental telegraph opened. Telegraphs could be sent even faster. And they were much cheaper to send, too.

Finish each sentence.

1. The Pony Express was a system that delivered mail on _____ .

2. Riders carried mail between _____ and California.

3. Bad _____ made it dangerous to carry the mail.

4. The Pony Express was replaced by the _____ .

Giant Giraffes

Giraffes are the tallest mammals on Earth. They are known for their long necks. Their legs are long too. Their legs are about six feet tall. That is taller than most adult humans! Giraffes are about 14–19 feet (4.2–5.8 m) tall.

This height helps giraffes survive. They can eat leaves from the tops of trees. Not too many animals can do that! So giraffes do not have to compete much for food. Giraffes can see a great distance. This helps them spot predators from far away. Because of this, they do not have many predators. However, lions and leopards do stalk giraffes sometimes.

Being so tall also has a downside. It is tough for giraffes to drink water. Bending down low is awkward. They are exposed in this position. This is when lions and leopards usually attack. Luckily, giraffes do not need to drink a lot! They get most of their water from the leaves they eat.

Even giraffe babies are huge. At birth, giraffes are about six feet (1.8 m) tall!

Read each sentence. Circle *true* or *false.*

1. Adult giraffes are usually six feet tall.	true	false
2. Giraffes do not have a lot of predators.	true	false
3. Giraffes need to drink a lot of water.	true	false
4. At birth, giraffes are only two feet tall.	true	false

Paul Revere's Nighttime Ride

In 1775, the British ruled over the American colonies. Many colonists wanted to be free from British rule. They were ready to rebel. This angered the British. The British army was stationed near Boston. The colonists watched the British army closely. They wanted to be ready for an attack.

The British planned to arrest some colonists. They wanted to arrest Samuel Adams and John Hancock. Some other colonists decided to warn Adams and Hancock. One of these colonists was named Paul Revere. On April 18, Revere rode a horse to Lexington, Massachusetts. He rode after dark so he would not be seen. He tried to be very quiet. He warned all the colonists about the British army's plan to attack. He warned Adams and Hancock too.

Then Revere kept riding. He rode toward Concord, Massachusetts. He wanted to warn the colonists there too. But Revere did not make it to Concord. The British captured him. They held a gun to Revere. They asked him questions about his ride.

Soon after, the Revolutionary War began. The first gunshots were fired in Lexington and Concord on April 19, 1775.

What's the order? Write 1, 2, 3, 4 on the lines.

_____ Paul Revere wanted to warn the colonists.

_____ The British army wanted to arrest some colonists.

_____ The Revolutionary War began.

_____ Colonists wanted to break away from the British.

The Solar System

We live on the planet Earth. Earth is part of the solar system. The solar system is like Earth's neighborhood.

The word "solar" means "related to the sun." The sun is at the center of the solar system. People used to think the sun moved around Earth. You can understand why. If you look into the sky, it sure looks like the sun moves! But some early astronomers rejected this idea. Nicolaus Copernicus was an astronomer in the 1500s. He was the first person to say that people were wrong. He believed Earth moved around the sun. In the 1600s, another astronomer named Galileo Galilei agreed. He built telescopes and observed the sky. He was convinced that Earth moved around the sun. This caused quite a stir! Galileo was arrested.

It turns out that these early astronomers were right! Earth revolves around the sun. So do seven other major planets. These are Mercury, Venus, Mars, Jupiter, Saturn, Uranus, and Neptune. That makes eight major planets. There is also one smaller planet called Pluto. Astronomers call Pluto a dwarf planet. Our solar system also includes moons, asteroids, and comets.

Finish each sentence.

1. Earth is part of a neighborhood called _____ .

2. The sun is at the _____ of the solar system.

3. People used to think _____ .

4. There are _____ major planets in our solar system.

Busy Little Bees!

What do you think about when you see a bee? Maybe you think about eating sweet honey. Maybe you worry the bee will sting you. But did you know that bees have a very important job? Bees are pollinators!

Pollination is how plants make new seeds. New seeds grow into new plants. Without pollination, we would not have as many plants. And we need plants! We eat them. We make clothing from them. They filter our air. Bees help the pollination of plants. But how?

Bees are attracted to the flowers of plants. They are attracted to the bright colors and sweet scents. They land on flowers to drink nectar. While they drink, pollen sticks to them. Pollen is a dust that plants make. The pollen is needed to make new seeds. When bees buzz away, pollen falls from their bodies. In this way, bees carry pollen from one part of the plant to another. And then seeds can form!

Bees are not the only pollinators. Other insects, birds, and bats also do the job. Not all plants need animals to pollinate. Wind or water can also carry pollen. But most of them rely on animals like busy little bees.

Read each question. Circle the right answer.

1. What is a bee's very important job?

   a) stinging people   b) pollinating flowers   c) buzzing around

2. What is pollen?   a) sweet honey   b) dust that plants make   c) nectar

3. What is pollination?

   a) how bees fly   b) how plants make seeds   c) how seeds grow

4. What are some pollinators besides bees?

   a) birds   b) wind   c) both (a) and (b)

16

Firefighters

Firefighters have important jobs. They keep communities safe.

Firefighters put out fires. They drive fire trucks to burning buildings. The trucks have long ladders and hoses. Firefighters climb the ladders to reach the buildings. They spray water on the fire. Firefighters drive fireboats to burning boats. Fireboats have pumps that pull water from a river, lake, or ocean. Firefighters spray this water on the fire. They fly helicopters to wildfires. Wildfires burn in nature. They can burn in forests or on mountains. Firefighters spray water from the helicopters onto the fire.

Firefighters save people and pets from fires. They have special gear to protect them. They wear flame-retardant coats and pants. They wear rubber boots and leather gloves. These clothes do not catch fire easily. Firefighters wear hard helmets to protect their heads. They wear masks so they do not breathe in smoke. They use an air tank to help them breathe.

Firefighters keep communities safe in other ways too. They visit schools and offices. They teach about fire safety. They teach about fire prevention. They drive ambulances. They help with medical emergencies. Firefighters are community helpers!

Read each sentence. Circle *true* or *false*.

1. Firefighters work to keep communities safe.	true	false
2. Firefighters drive burning boats.	true	false
3. Firefighters wear special gear to protect them.	true	false
4. Firefighters help with medical emergencies.	true	false

Ring of Fire

Volcanoes are a kind of mountain. Inside, magma sits under the surface of Earth. Magma is liquid rock. Sometimes volcanoes erupt. Magma explodes from inside the volcano. Once magma flows out of the volcano, it is called lava. Lava is very hot. It can get up to 2,282 degrees Fahrenheit!

Most volcanoes on Earth are in the Ring of Fire. This is an area around the Pacific Ocean. Some volcanoes are even under the ocean!

There are three stages of volcanic eruptions. Extinct volcanoes have not erupted for thousands of years. Dormant volcanoes have not erupted in a long time. Active volcanoes have erupted more recently. There are about 1,500 active volcanoes on Earth. The largest active volcano is Mauna Loa in Hawaii. Mauna Loa's last eruption started in 1984 and is still happening today.

Volcanoes are dangerous! When lava flows, it burns everything in its path. Volcanoes can set off mudslides and rock slides. They can cause floods, tsunamis, and earthquakes. But the soil near volcanoes is very fertile. Some of the best coffee grows near Mauna Loa.

Answer the questions below.

1. What is magma called after it leaves the volcano?

_____

2. Around what ocean are most volcanoes located?

_____

3. Where is Earth's biggest active volcano?

_____

4. What is one good thing about volcanoes?

_____

Community Gardens

Community gardens are popular in cities. Many city homes do not have outdoor space. People in cities often cannot grow a garden at home. So they share a community garden with neighbors!

Community garden members often pay dues. Dues pay for upkeep of the garden. Dues might pay for mulch to cover garden paths. In some community gardens, members work together. They plant one big garden. They all care for the plants. They share the vegetables that grow. In other community gardens, each member has a small plot of land. They each plant their own garden. They each care for their own garden. They keep all of the vegetables that grow in the plot.

Some community gardens are open to the public. Only members can care for the gardens. Only members can eat the vegetables that grow. But anyone can enter these gardens. Anyone can enjoy their beauty. Other community gardens are open only to their members. Only members can enter these gardens.

Either way, community gardens are a shared space. They are a place to meet neighbors. They are a place to work together. They help create a sense of community!

Read each sentence. Circle *true* or *false*.

1. Community garden members often pay dues.	true	false
2. Different community gardens have different rules.	true	false
3. All community gardens are open to the public.	true	false
4. Neighbors share community gardens.	true	false

"The Star-Spangled Banner"

You probably know the national anthem. It is called "The Star-Spangled Banner." You probably have heard it sung before a big sports game. What is the song about? Who wrote it?

During the Revolutionary War, the United States declared independence from Great Britain. But Great Britain still interfered with the United States. So they went to war again. The War of 1812 lasted for more than two and a half years.

In September of 1814, the British attacked Fort McHenry. Fort McHenry is in Baltimore, Maryland. An American lawyer named Francis Scott Key saw the attack. He was on a warship in Baltimore Harbor. He watched the battle all night. He saw rockets and bombs explode. The Americans won the battle! Key saw that an American flag had lots of holes in it. But it was still waving! He felt proud of his country.

Key wrote a poem about the battle. He called it "Defence of Fort M'Henry." Later, the poem was put to music. The name was changed to "The Star-Spangled Banner." In 1931, Congress declared the song to be the national anthem.

Read each question. Circle the right answer.

1. Who did the United States fight against during the War of 1812?

   a) Great Britain   b) Baltimore, Maryland   c) Fort McHenry

2. From where did Francis Scott Key watch the battle at Fort McHenry?

   a) on a warship   b) in the Baltimore Harbor   c) both (a) and (b)

3. After the battle, how did Francis Scott Key feel about his country?

   a) scared   b) sad   c) glad

4. When did Congress choose the national anthem?   a) 1812   b) 1931   c) 1814

Big Birds

Ostriches are the biggest living birds. They grow up to nine feet (2.7 m) tall. They can weigh more than 350 pounds (158 kg). But their wings are very small. They do not use their wings to fly. Ostriches are too heavy to fly! Instead, they run. They use their wings for balance. Ostriches have long legs. Their legs are very strong. They can run fast for a long time.

Ostriches live in the African desert. They have many predators. Some of these are lions, leopards, cheetahs, and hyenas. Ostriches usually run away from predators. Sometimes, they use their strong legs to kick predators. These powerful kicks can kill even a fierce lion!

Other times, ostriches hide from predators. What if there is nowhere to hide? Ostriches will lie down in the desert sand. Their legs, neck, and head blend into the sand. From far away, it looks like the ostriches have buried their heads!

Ostrich babies are big too. One ostrich egg is the size of 24 chicken eggs! When an egg hatches, the baby is as big as an adult chicken. When the baby is 18 months old, it is already full-grown!

Finish each sentence.

1. Ostriches use their wings for _____ .

2. Ostriches use their strong legs to _____ .

3. Ostriches lie down in the sand to _____ from predators.

4. Ostrich babies are as big as _____ .

Lewis and Clark

The United States is a big country. It used to be much smaller. In 1803, President Thomas Jefferson bought land from the French. The land doubled the size of the country. Jefferson did not know what that land looked like. He asked two men to travel west to explore.

On May 14, 1804, Meriwether Lewis and William Clark began the adventure! They brought a team of more than 30 men. They brought a lot of supplies. They did not know what to expect. Lewis and Clark started in Missouri. They traveled to the Pacific Ocean and back. The trip took almost two and a half years! It was a long, hard adventure. There were a lot of rivers and mountains. Sometimes it was very hard to cross them.

Lewis and Clark wrote a lot of notes during the trip. They wrote about different plants and animals. They drew maps. They also met a lot of Native Americans. One Native American woman even joined their trip. Her name was Sacagawea. Sacagawea helped Lewis and Clark. She taught them which plants were safe to eat. She helped them talk to other Native Americans. Jefferson was happy with Lewis and Clark's exploration.

Answer the questions below.

1. Where did Lewis and Clark start their trip?

_____

2. What did Lewis and Clark bring on their trip?

_____

3. How long did Lewis and Clark's trip take to complete?

_____

4. Name one way that Sacagawea helped Lewis and Clark.

_____

Don't Catch a Cold!

It is no fun to catch a cold. Your nose runs. It gets stuffy. You sneeze. Your head feels clogged. You feel awful! Colds are easy to catch. They are also easy to prevent. You just have to know how!

A healthy lifestyle can help you stay healthy. Be sure to eat lots of different good-for-you foods. Drink a lot of water. Get plenty of sleep each night. And stay active! Be sure to run and jump outside each day. A healthy body is better at keeping colds away.

Sometimes cold germs are all around you. Maybe your dad, sister, or best friend has a cold. How can you prevent catching it? First, wash your hands a lot. Be sure to use warm water and soap. Rub your soapy hands together for 30 seconds. How long is 30 seconds? Sing "Happy Birthday" two times. Then rinse and dry your hands. Avoid touching your eyes. It is easy for cold germs to get into your body through your eyes. Do not share forks, spoons, or cups with anyone. Finally, cough or sneeze into the inside of your elbow instead of into your hands. This helps prevent sharing any germs you may already have!

Read each sentence. Circle *true* or *false*.

1. Colds are difficult to catch.	true	false
2. Getting plenty of sleep helps you prevent catching a cold.	true	false
3. You do not need to use soap when you wash hands.	true	false
4. Coughing or sneezing into your hands is a good idea.	true	false

Phases of the Moon

The moon seems to glow with light. But the moon is thought to be a big rock. It does not make any light. The light we see on the moon is sunlight. Sunlight reflects off half of the moon. We do not see all of this light every night. The moon moves around Earth. When it moves, the amount of sunlight we can see changes. This is called the phases of the moon.

There are eight phases of the moon. It takes one month to finish the cycle. These are the phases of the moon:

new moon
waxing crescent
first quarter
waxing gibbous
full moon
waning gibbous
third quarter
waning crescent

During the new moon, we do not see any light from the moon. The sky looks dark. Then the moon appears to grow. This is called waxing. The moon waxes until it is a full moon. During the full moon, we see all of the light. The moon looks like a circle. Then the moon appears to shrink. This is called waning. In between, we see gibbous, quarter, and crescent moons. The crescent moon looks like a smile. The quarter moon looks like a semicircle. The gibbous moon is between a semicircle and full circle.

Draw a line from each moon phase to its shape.

full moon	semicircle
crescent moon	smile
quarter moon	no light
new moon	circle

California Gold Rush

In 1848, a man found gold in California. His name was James Marshall. Marshall was building a sawmill with John Sutter. He saw flakes of gold floating in the water. Marshall told Sutter about the gold. Soon, news of the gold spread. By 1849, people all over the world knew about the gold. People from every continent rushed to California. They were called the forty-niners. Between 1848 and 1855, there were more than 300,000 forty-niners. Everyone wanted to find gold!

When someone found gold, others set up camp nearby. Some of these camps turned into towns. They were called boomtowns because they grew so quickly. One of these boomtowns is San Francisco. When the gold rush started, there were 1,000 people living in San Francisco. Just a few years later, there were 36,000 people living there! San Francisco is still a big city.

Other boomtowns did not last long. As soon as the gold ran out, the forty-niners left. As soon as the forty-niners left, businesses closed. These places became ghost towns. Some ghost towns still exist. You can visit them and see the old, empty buildings!

Finish each sentence.

1. People rushed to _____ to find gold.

2. People looking for gold were called _____.

3. _____ were towns that grew very quickly.

4. Towns that were abandoned after the gold rush are called _____.

Ant Colonies

Ants are social insects. They live in organized communities. These communities are called colonies. Everything ants do serves the needs of their colony.

Each ant in a colony has a special job. A female is the leader of the colony. She is called the queen. The queen lays eggs to make ant babies. All baby ants in a colony hatch from the queen's eggs. A queen ant can live for up to 30 years. That means her colony can last for a long time!

The rest of the female ants in a colony cannot lay eggs. These female ants are called the worker ants. The worker ants do a lot to help the colony. They care for eggs until they hatch. They find and store food. They build a nest for the colony. The nests can be very complex. They have many rooms. The queen has her own room. There is a room for eggs. There is a room for food storage, and so on. Worker ants live about one to three years.

Male ants are called drones. Their only job is to mate with the queen. Male ants only live for a few weeks.

Answer the questions below.

1. Which ant lays eggs in a colony?

_____

2. Are worker ants male or female?

_____

3. Who finds food for the colony?

_____

4. What is the job of drone ants?

_____

Grand Canyon

The Grand Canyon is in Arizona. It is a giant hole in the ground. The canyon is so big that you can see it from space!

The walls of the Grand Canyon are rock. Erosion created the canyon. Water from the Colorado River wore away the rock. It took a long time for this to happen. Scientists say it started 17 million years ago! The river is still eroding the canyon today.

There are a lot of layers in the rock. There is a different kind of rock in each layer. The rock at the bottom of the canyon is called schist. It is two billion years old! There are fossils of trilobites in the rocks. Trilobites lived in the river 500 million years ago. They are related to horseshoe crabs.

Today, there are other animals that live in the canyon. The higher levels are forests and meadows. Wild turkeys and mule deer live there. The climate gets drier farther down. The lowest level is a desert. There are cacti, scorpions, and rattlesnakes.

Read each question. Circle the right answer.

1. Where is the Grand Canyon?

   a) in space   **b)** Arizona   **c)** Colorado

2. How many years ago did water start eroding the canyon?

   a) 17 million   **b)** two billion   **c)** 500 million

3. What kind of rock is the Canyon made out of?

   a) schist   **b)** fossils   **c)** many different rocks

4. Which animal lives at the highest level of the canyon?

   a) rattlesnake   **b)** mule   **c)** mule deer

Penicillin

Penicillin is a common antibiotic. An antibiotic is a drug that kills bacteria. Some bacteria cause infections. Doctors use antibiotics to treat these infections. Penicillin can treat strep throat or an ear infection.

In 1928, a Scottish scientist discovered penicillin by accident! His name was Alexander Fleming. Fleming was studying one kind of bacteria. He put the bacteria in some petri dishes. Then he went on vacation. When Fleming came back, he made his discovery. Mold was growing in some of the petri dishes. The mold had killed the bacteria! Fleming tested the mold. It killed many kinds of bacteria. Later, other scientists built on Fleming's discovery. They turned the mold into a drug. In the 1940s, penicillin was used to treat a lot of people. It is still used today.

Fleming's discovery was very exciting. Before that, people knew that bacteria caused infections. But no one knew how to cure them. No one knew how to kill bacteria without hurting the person. Penicillin changed that. Penicillin has saved millions of lives. Fleming was a hero all because of an accident!

What's the order? Write 1, 2, 3, 4 on the lines.

_____ Alexander Fleming was studying bacteria.

_____ Penicillin is used to treat bacterial infections.

_____ Alexander Fleming saw mold growing in his petri dishes.

_____ Scientists turned mold into a drug.

Earth Day

Earth Day is a holiday to celebrate our world. It started in the United States. In the 1960s, Senator Gaylord Nelson cared about keeping Earth healthy. He wanted the government to protect Earth. So Nelson started Earth Day. He wanted to teach people how to care for our world. He wanted the government to see that people cared about Earth.

The first official Earth Day was on April 22, 1970. More than 20 million Americans celebrated. Now, people in 192 countries celebrate Earth Day each year! On Earth Day, we learn how to protect our world. We learn how to keep it clean. We try to reduce pollution. We try to conserve energy.

How can you celebrate Earth Day? Clean up the litter at a park. Ride your bike or walk. Cars and buses make lots of air pollution! Plant a new tree. Separate your recycling from the trash. Turn off the lights when you leave a room. There are a lot of ways to celebrate our world. But most of all, remember to do these things every day. Consider every day to be Earth Day!

Finish each sentence.

1. _____ wanted the government to protect Earth.

2. More than 20 million _____ celebrated the first Earth Day.

3. On Earth Day, we try to reduce _____ and conserve _____ .

4. You can celebrate Earth Day by cleaning up _____ .

Benjamin Franklin

Today we use electric lights. But electricity is a modern invention. Benjamin Franklin lived in the 1700s. During his life, people used candles for light. No one used electricity. They did not know a lot about it.

Franklin wanted to learn more about electricity. He studied it a lot. Franklin thought lightning was electricity. He wanted to prove it. In 1752, Franklin did an experiment. He flew a kite during a lightning storm. There was a metal key tied to the kite. The key picked up some sparks from the lightning. Franklin trapped the sparks in a special jar. He studied the sparks in the jar. He proved the sparks were electricity. Lightning is electricity from a storm!

Franklin was excited about his discovery. He studied lightning and electricity more. He invented the lightning rod. Lightning rods are tall metal rods that sit on top of buildings. If lightning strikes a building, the building can catch on fire. Lightning rods protect the building. Lightning strikes the rod instead of the building. The electricity goes from the rod into the ground. We still use lightning rods today!

Answer the questions below.

1. In the 1700s, what did people use for light?

_____

2. What did the key do in Benjamin Franklin's kite experiment?

_____

3. What did Benjamin Franklin prove about lightning?

_____

4. What did Benjamin Franklin invent that we still use today?

_____

American Alligators

American alligators live in the southeastern United States. They are common in Florida and Louisiana. They can walk on land. But their legs are short. They are a bit clumsy. Alligators are much better in water. Their webbed feet and strong tails help them swim. Alligators live in rivers, lakes, and swamps. But they cannot breathe under the water! They need to come up for air.

People like to hunt alligators. They use their skin to make leather. They eat their meat. But they were hunting too many alligators. American alligators were almost extinct. This means there were few American alligators left in the world. In 1967, they were put on a special list to protect them. It was illegal to hunt alligators. Then the alligators started multiplying. Now there are more than a million American alligators living!

People often confuse alligators with crocodiles. But they are different! There are some ways to tell them apart. Alligators are darker than crocodiles. They have shorter, wider heads. Alligators only live in fresh water. Some crocodiles live in salt water. Alligators are calmer than crocodiles.

Read each sentence. Circle *true* or *false*.

1. Alligators are good swimmers.	true	false
2. Alligators were almost extinct because people hunted them.	true	false
3. Crocodiles and alligators are the same.	true	false
4. Alligators live in salt water.	true	false

The American Flag

Every country in the world has a national flag. The colors and pictures on each flag mean different things. They send a message about the country.

The first official American flag was made in 1777. The British used to rule American colonists. The colonists opposed this rule. The colonists formed the United States in 1776. The new country needed a national flag. Many people believe Betsy Ross sewed the first American flag.

The first American national flag had 13 red and white stripes. It had 13 white stars set on blue. The mix of red, white, and blue sent a message of revolution and freedom. This made sense for the American flag in 1777. Americans had just opposed British rule. They had just won their freedom. The new country had 13 colonies. So the flag had 13 stars and 13 stripes. Today's flag is only a little different. The colors are the same. There are still 13 stripes. But now there are more stars. There is one star for each state in the United States. That means there are 50 stars on today's flag!

Finish each sentence.

1. Every country has a _____ flag.

2. The first American flag had 13 white _____ set on blue.

3. The colors on the American flag send a message of _____

_____ .

4. Today there are _____ stars on the American flag.

Rainbow Eucalyptus Tree

Most trees have brown bark. But not the rainbow eucalyptus tree! The rainbow eucalyptus lives up to its name. Its bark is a rainbow of colors. It looks like an artist painted the bark. But it is natural!

Trees shed their bark. New bark grows from the inside of the tree. This makes the tree thicker. After a while, the tree is too thick for the old bark. The old bark peels off of the tree.

The rainbow eucalyptus tree sheds brown bark. But the bark underneath is not brown. The new bark is bright green! The new bark ages over time. The bark changes color as it ages. The bright green bark turns dark green. Then it turns blue and then purple. The purple bark turns pink and then orange. Finally, the orange bark turns dark red-brown. Then it sheds again! The shedding does not happen all at once. So the tree shows many colors at one time. The tree looks like it has been painted with long, wavy lines. It is very beautiful!

People often use rainbow eucalyptus trees to make paper. Surprisingly, the paper is not so colorful. Pulp from these trees makes white paper!

Read each sentence. Circle *true* or *false*.

1. Artists paint the bark of rainbow eucalyptus trees.	true	false
2. Rainbow eucalyptus trees shed their bark.	true	false
3. The shedding happens all at once.	true	false
4. Rainbow eucalyptus trees make colorful paper.	true	false

The National Parks

National parks are special parks. The land in these parks is largely untouched. This means that no one changed it. Most areas in a national park are just like you would find them in nature. There are not many buildings or sidewalks or playgrounds. The land you see in a national park is natural.

In each country, the government runs its national parks. It makes sure that no one changes the parks. The government guards the land. No one can destroy the land. Animals can live happily in their natural homes.

But people can still enjoy these parks! People visit national parks to enjoy their beauty. They can hike and camp in the parks. They can snorkel and kayak. They can ski. They can see geysers and volcanoes. There is a lot of history in the parks too. People can visit old battlefields and historic homes. They can see ancient drawings on rock walls.

The world's first national park in the United States was Yellowstone National Park. It became a national park in 1872. Yellowstone National Park is in Wyoming in the United States. There are 401 national parks in the United States!

Answer the questions below.

1. What is special about a national park?

_____

2. Who runs national parks?

_____

3. Are people allowed to go to national parks?

_____

4. Where is the world's first national park?

_____

Volunteering in Your Community

Being a part of a community feels good! How can you feel like part of the group? One way is to volunteer. Use your time and energy to help the people in your community.

There are many ways to get involved. One way is to help keep your neighborhood clean. Take a walk around the block. Or visit to a nearby park. Throw away any litter you find. Be sure to wear gloves. That way, you will not catch germs!

Visit a nursing home. Many people at nursing homes love when kids visit. Some of them do not have their own grandchildren. Ask the nursing home to match you with someone. Play games together. Read books together. Visit often!

Food banks collect food. They give the food to people who cannot buy their own. Help a grown-up shop for food. Bring the food to a food bank!

Go to a nearby animal shelter. The animals there need extra love and attention. Spend time playing with the animals. Give them lots of snuggles. Maybe you can even help walk some of the dogs!

Finish each sentence.

1. It is important to wear gloves when you clean up litter so you do not catch _____ .

2. Many people in nursing homes like seeing kids. Some do not have their own _____ .

3. _____ give food to people who cannot buy their own.

4. Animals at animal shelters need extra _____ and _____ .

Abraham Lincoln

Abraham Lincoln was the 16th president of the United States. He led the country from 1861 to 1865. But the United States was at war. The Civil War was a fight between the North and the South. The United States almost became two countries. Lincoln fought to keep the North and the South together.

The Southern states did not like Lincoln's ideas. Lincoln thought slaves should be free. People in the South wanted to keep their slaves. When Lincoln became the president, the Southern states decided to secede. This means that they decided to break away from the United States. They wanted to form a new country.

South Carolina was the first state to secede. Ten more states followed. These states formed the Confederacy.

The Northern states were called the Union. Lincoln wanted the Union and the Confederacy to be one country again. The Civil War was very bloody. A lot of people died. But in the end, Lincoln and the Union won! The United States was one country again. And Lincoln put an end to slavery.

But Lincoln still had enemies. John Wilkes Booth was from the Confederacy. Soon after the Civil War was over, Booth killed Lincoln.

Read each question. Circle the right answer.

1. Who was fighting the Confederacy during the Civil War?

    a) The South   b) Lincoln   c) The Union

2. Whom did Abraham Lincoln want to set free?

    a) the Southern states   b) slaves   c) John Wilkes Booth

3. The Southern states wanted to secede from the United States. What does *secede* mean?   a) end slavery   b) fight   c) break away

4. Who won the Civil War? a) The North   b) John Wilkes Booth   c) The South

Using a Compass

It is fun to hike in nature. But it is easy to get turned around. Which way is which? Nature does not have street signs to help. How can you find your way?

A compass is a great tool. A compass tells you which way is which! The needle of a compass always points north.

How does a compass know which way is north? It uses magnets! Every magnet has two poles. One side is the north pole. The other side is the south pole. Two north poles push away from each other. Two south poles push away from each other. But a north pole and a south pole pull toward each other.

Earth is naturally magnetic. The south pole of the magnet is near the North Pole of Earth. The north pole of the magnet is near the South Pole of Earth.

The needle of a compass is a tiny magnet. So the north pole of the needle pulls toward the South Pole of Earth's magnet. This means the needle points toward the North Pole.

It sounds a little confusing. Just remember that the needle of a compass always points north. Then you can find your way!

Finish each sentence.

1. The needle of a compass always points _____ .

2. Every magnet has two _____ .

3. The north pole of one magnet and the south pole of another
   magnet _____ each other.

4. The _____ pole of a compass's needle points to Earth's North Pole.

Hula

Hula is a kind of music and dance. It started in Hawaii. Hawaiians use hula to tell stories. It is part of their rich oral tradition.

When hula started, Hawaiians used it to pass on history. They used it to pass on the stories of their people. Parents taught children through hula.

Hula music started with chanting. Chanting is a special kind of singing. Hawaiians also used some native instruments. They played gourd drums to keep a beat. They played bamboo sticks. In the 19th century, hula music started changing. Western people brought European instruments to Hawaii. Hawaiians learned to play guitars and ukuleles. The chants turned into songs.

Hula dance is an important part of the storytelling. Hula dancers sway their hips. They stomp their feet. But their hands tell the true story. There are hand motions that show parts of nature. There are hand motions that mean flower or rain. There are hand motions that show feelings, like longing.

Hawaiians also perform hula for travelers. This is not true Hawaiian hula. Most travelers do not understand the stories. The travelers just like a good show!

Read each sentence. Circle *true* or *false*.

1. Hawaiians use hula to tell stories.	true	false
2. The first hula music used guitars and ukuleles.	true	false
3. Hula dancers use their hands to show feelings.	true	false
4. Travelers like hula shows because they see true Hawaiian hula.	true	false

Hurricanes

Hurricanes are really powerful storms. They have strong winds. They have a lot of rain. They can cause ocean waters to flood nearby land. Hurricanes can destroy buildings. They can destroy cars and trees. They can even kill people!

Hurricanes always start over the ocean. But they do not happen just anywhere! The ocean water has to be very warm. The water moves up into the storm. The hurricane gets stronger and stronger. As the storm spins, it can move toward land.

When a hurricane moves over land, it starts to slow down. It starts to lose strength. But it takes time for the hurricane to die out. It still has time to destroy the land below. A hurricane usually lasts more than a week!

We give hurricanes people names! Most kinds of storms end quickly. But hurricanes last for so long. Weather scientists track them. News reporters update people about them. It is easier to talk about them if they have names.

Read each question. Circle the right answer.

1. What does a hurricane destroy?

   a) buildings   b) trees   c) both (a) and (b)

2. Where do hurricanes start?

   a) over cold ocean water   b) over warm ocean water   c) over land

3. How long do hurricanes last?

   a) 80 days   b) more than a week   c) a short time

4. Why do we name hurricanes?

   a) to make it easier to talk about them   b) to make them seem like people

   c) to help them end quickly

First Transcontinental Railroad

It takes six hours to fly from New York to California. But the trip across the country was not always so quick. Before the 1860s, it could take six months to make the trip! People traveled in horse-drawn wagons. It was a difficult journey. Bad weather and wild animals made it unsafe. Robbers caused problems for travelers too.

In 1862, President Abraham Lincoln signed an act to build a railroad. There were already railroads in the country. But there were no transcontinental railroads. That is, there were no railroads that went across the whole country. Lincoln's act gave railroad companies land. It paid the companies to build the track.

Building the track was hard work! Bad weather got in the way. The workers had to blast tunnels through mountains. The railroad was built through Native American land. The Native Americans were angry. There were fights between workers and Native Americans. It took about six years to build the whole railroad! The workers finished on May 10, 1869.

The transcontinental railroad made the trip across the country safer. It also made the trip shorter. Now people could travel from New York to California in one week!

Answer the questions below.

1. How long did it take people to travel from New York to California before the 1860s? _____

2. Why were Native Americans angry about the transcontinental railroad?

   _____

3. When did workers finish building the transcontinental railroad?

   _____

4. How long did it take people to travel from New York to California on the transcontinental railroad?

   _____

Honeybees

Honeybees are special kinds of bees. They make honey! No other bug makes food that people eat.

Bees do not make honey for us, though. They make it for them! Bees eat pollen from flowers. They drink nectar from flowers. But there are no flowers in winter. What do the bees eat then? They eat honey!

Worker bees fly from flower to flower. They collect pollen and nectar. They bring this food back to the hive. They feed some pollen to bee babies. They store some of it for winter. They use the nectar to make honey.

Bees have two stomachs. They use one to eat their food. They use the other to store nectar. Back at the hive, the bees throw up the nectar! Then they fan it with their wings. This helps to dry it. The result is honey! The bees keep the honey stored in the hive to use later.

Different kinds of honey taste different. The flavor of the honey depends on where the bees got the nectar. Nectar from different flowers makes honey with different flavors.

What's the order? Write 1, 2, 3, 4 on the lines.

_____ Bees throw up the nectar.

_____ Bees drink the nectar from flowers.

_____ Bees fan the nectar with their wings.

_____ Bees store the nectar in their second stomachs.

Simple Machines

All machines can be made from six simple machines. Simple machines are basic tools. They help us push or pull. They make doing work easier. The chart below shows information about simple machines.

SIMPLE MACHINE	DESCRIPTION	EXAMPLE
Lever	A bar that turns on a fulcrum	A seesaw is a lever. The fulcrum supports the seesaw in the middle. One side goes down. The other side goes up.
Inclined plane	A ramp	A dump truck uses an inclined plane. The truck bed tips. The dirt spills out.
Screw	An inclined plane that wraps around a rod	A jar uses a screw. It keeps the lid on tight.
Wedge	Thick on one side with a sharp edge on the other	A doorstop is a wedge. It holds open a door.
Wheel and axle	A wheel that spins around a rod	A doorknob is a wheel and axle. The knobs are two wheels. The rod that connects them is the axle.
Pulley	A wheel with a rope around it	A flagpole uses a pulley. It raises and lowers a flag.

Draw a line from each simple machine to an example of that type of machine.

lever	flagpole
inclined plane	dump truck
screw	seesaw
wedge	doorstop
wheel and axle	doorknob
pulley	jar lid

Sharks and Remoras

Sharks and remoras have a special kind of friendship. It is called a symbiotic relationship. This means that sharks and remoras help each other.

Remoras are small fish that live in the ocean. They live where the water is warm. Remoras are also called suckerfish. They have a disk on top of their heads. The disk can stick to things by sucking. Remoras use this sucker to stick to other animals. It is common for remoras to stay with sharks. They stick their suckers to a shark's belly.

Remoras can swim by themselves. But they like to work with sharks. Sharks help the remoras. Sharks protect remoras from other predators. Remoras also eat leftovers from the sharks' meals.

Remoras help sharks too. They keep the sharks clean and healthy. They eat parasites from the sharks' skin and teeth. Parasites use sharks for their own gain. But they do not help the sharks. Parasites harm the sharks. It is a big help when remoras eat the parasites!

Even so, sharks do not always seem to like remoras. Remoras move around a lot to find the best position. It seems to bother a lot of sharks.

Answer the questions below.

1. Sharks and remoras have a symbiotic relationship. What does this mean?

_____

2. What is another name for remoras?

_____

3. How do sharks help remoras?

_____

4. How do remoras help sharks?

_____

Antarctica

Antarctica is a continent. It is all the way south on Earth. The South Pole is on Antarctica. It is very cold there! The coldest temperature ever recorded on Earth was in Antarctica. In 1983, the temperature was −128.6 degrees F (−89.2 degrees C)! Almost the whole continent is covered in thick ice. Most of the world's ice is in Antarctica.

Very few people live on Antarctica. People who live there are scientists. The living conditions are very harsh for people. It is too cold. It is too windy. And it is too dry. In fact, Antarctica is a desert! We usually think of deserts as hot places. But a desert is just a place where there is very little rain or snowfall.

Other animals are able to live there though. Emperor penguins live in Antarctica. So do seals. There is also some plant life on Antarctica. There are many kinds of mosses and liverworts that grow. But they can only grow in a small area of the continent. And the plants only grow for a few days or weeks in the summer.

Read each sentence. Circle *true* or *false*.

1. Antarctica is covered in thick ice.	true	false
2. Humans easily get used to Antarctica's weather.	true	false
3. Antarctica gets a lot of snowfall.	true	false
4. Plants can only grow in Antarctica for a very short time.	true	false

How to Make Recycled Paper

Today, most paper is made from trees. A lot of trees are chopped down to make paper. Recycling paper saves trees. This turns old paper into new paper. New trees do not need to be chopped down.

You can make your own recycled paper! Collect scrap paper. This can be any paper you do not need anymore. You can use junk mail. You can use old newspapers. Tear the scrap paper into tiny pieces. Soak the pieces in hot water for a few hours. The paper will get very soggy! Put a few handfuls of the paper into a blender. Fill the blender half up with water. Blend until the paper is very mushy. Ask a grown-up for help!

Pour some water into a rectangular pan. Fit a piece of window screen into the pan. Spread the paper mush evenly over the screen. Lift the screen out of the pan. Place it on a towel to drain. Place another towel on top of the paper mush. Roll a rolling pin over the towel. This will flatten the paper and squeeze out extra water. Let the paper dry for 24 hours. Your recycled paper is ready to use!

What's the order? Write 1, 2, 3, 4 on the lines.

_____ Roll a rolling pin over the towel on the paper.

_____ Put paper into blender.

_____ Spread wet paper over a screen.

_____ Tear scrap paper into tiny pieces.

Harriet Tubman and the Underground Railroad

The Underground Railroad was not really underground. It was not really a railroad. It was a way for slaves to escape to freedom. It was called "underground" because it was a secret. It was called a railroad because the slaves traveled from one place to another.

In the early 1800s, the South counted on slavery. But slavery was illegal in some northern states. Slavery was illegal in Canada too. A lot of slaves wanted to escape from the South. They wanted to head north to be free.

Many people wanted to end slavery. But it was dangerous work. It was illegal to help slaves escape. These people could be hanged! For safety, they used railroad words as a code. Stations were houses where slaves could hide. Conductors led slaves along the path.

One famous conductor was Harriet Tubman. Tubman was born a slave. In 1849, she traveled on the Underground Railroad to escape. She reached freedom in Pennsylvania. Then she worked as a conductor for eight years. Tubman helped more than 300 slaves escape!

Read each sentence. Circle *true* or *false*.

1. The Underground Railroad was an escape path for slaves.	true	false
2. The Underground Railroad used trains for travel.	true	false
3. Stations were houses where slave catchers lived.	true	false
4. Harriet Tubman was a conductor on the Underground Railroad.	true	false

Platypuses

Have you ever seen a platypus? It is a very strange-looking animal! In fact, the first scientists that saw one thought it was a trick! A platypus looks like a mix of animals. It has a body and fur like an otter. It has a tail like a beaver. It has a bill and webbed feet like a duck. It is a mammal, but it lays eggs.

Platypuses live in Australia. They are very good swimmers. They use their front feet to paddle. They use their back feet and tail to steer. They hunt for food underwater. They scoop up bugs, worms, and shellfish with their bills. They store the food in their cheeks. They eat the food once they are out of the water.

Platypuses can run on land too. They pull back the webbing on their feet. Their nails come out. This helps them run. Platypuses also use their nails to dig. They build dens near the edge of the water. Male platypuses have sharp stingers on their back feet. They use these to poison enemies.

Platypuses have been around for a long time. Their oldest relatives lived 112 million years ago. They lived with the dinosaurs!

Finish each sentence.

1. Platypuses are _____, but they lay eggs.

2. Platypuses use their front feet to _____ .

3. Male platypuses have _____ on their back feet.

4. Relatives of platypuses lived with the _____ .

Kwanzaa

Kwanzaa is an African American holiday. It starts on December 26. It lasts for seven days. Kwanzaa is not a religious holiday. It honors African American culture.

Dr. Maulana Karenga started Kwanzaa in 1966. Karenga worried that African Americans did not connect to their African roots. He wanted to help them feel proud of their roots.

There are seven values of Kwanzaa. Each night, families light a candle. Then they talk about one of the values. The values build up family, community, and culture.

People decorate their houses in red, black, and green. They display African art. They wear African-style clothing.

The name "Kwanzaa" comes from Swahili words. Swahili is one of the main languages in Africa. The words mean "first fruits of the harvest." Kwanzaa is based on an African harvest festival. There is a big feast on December 31. The feast is called karamu. During karamu, people dance. They tell stories. They exchange gifts. It is a very joyous time!

Answer the questions below.

1. Why did Dr. Maulana Karenga start Kwanzaa?

_____

2. What is the purpose of the seven values of Kwanzaa?

_____

3. What are the colors of Kwanzaa?

_____

4. What is the name of Kwanzaa's big feast?

_____

Constellations

A constellation is a group of stars that forms a picture. It is like playing Connect the Dots! The pictures are of animals, people, and objects. Each constellation has a story.

One well-known constellation is Orion. Orion is a hunter. He is named after a hunter in an old Greek story. Orion is a winter constellation. He shows from late fall to early spring.

Constellations were useful a long time ago. They helped people track the seasons. If you could see Orion, it must be winter! This helped people know when to plant and harvest crops.

Constellations also helped people find their way. Many people used the North Star to know where they were. The North Star is part of the Ursa Minor constellation. "Ursa Minor" means "small bear." It is easier to find the North Star if you look for a picture of a bear!

There are 88 constellations. A Greek astronomer named Ptolemy described 48 of them. He lived from 90 to 168 CE. Constellations have been around for a long time! There are also 40 newer constellations.

Look at the night sky. Try connecting the dots. Make up your own constellations!

Read each sentence. Circle *true* or *false*.

1. Constellations are groups of stars that form pictures.	true	false
2. Orion is seen year-round.	true	false
3. The North Star is part of a constellation of a bear.	true	false
4. There are 40 constellations in the sky.	true	false

The Statue of Liberty

The Statue of Liberty is a symbol of freedom and democracy. But did you know it came from France? The French wanted to honor America. The Statue of Liberty was a birthday gift from France!

A sculptor named Frédéric-Auguste Bartholdi planned the Statue of Liberty. It took 21 years before the statue stood in America. The French raised money to build it. Then they built it. They shipped it to America in pieces. The statue's torch stood in Madison Square Park in New York City. It stood there for six years! Americans raised money to build the base. Finally, in 1886, the base and the statue were done. They were put on Bedloe's Island in New York Harbor. It is now called Liberty Island.

You can visit the Statue of Liberty. She is huge! Her face alone is over 17 feet (5 m) tall. That is about as tall as a giraffe! Inside the statue, you can climb up to the crown. There are 354 stairs to the top! The statue weighs 225 tons (204.1 t). That is equal to about 110 cars. Even though Lady Liberty is so heavy, she sways in the wind!

Answer the questions below.

1. What is the Statue of Liberty a sign of?

_____

2. What artist planned the statue?

_____

3. Where does the Statue of Liberty stand?

_____

4. How high can you climb inside the Statue of Liberty?

_____

Endangered Animals

An endangered animal is in danger of becoming extinct. This means no more of that animal will live on Earth. That kind of animal will disappear forever! Animals are considered endangered when there are very few of them left.

There are many things that endanger animals. Sometimes predators kill too many of them. Sometimes disease kills too many of them. Sometimes there is not enough food for the animals. Global warming is changing weather patterns. These changes can endanger animals too. Often, people endanger animals. We hunt them. We use them for scientific studies.

When animals become extinct, the balance of nature changes. That animal's predators do not have enough food. The extinct animal's food supply increases. After all, that animal is not around to keep eating! This could mean there are too many of another kind of animal.

The government protects endangered animals. It enacts laws against hunting those animals, for example. Sometimes they are successful! One success story is our national bird. The bald eagle was endangered in the 1960s. Dangerous pesticides were killing the babies. The government outlawed the pesticides. They helped the eagles breed. Now the number of living bald eagles is much bigger!

Write a cause or effect to each item on the chart.

	CAUSE	EFFECT
1	Global warming is changing weather patterns.	
2	People hunt animals too much.	
3		The animal's predator does not have enough food.
4		Some animals are no longer endangered.

Susan B. Anthony

Susan B. Anthony was a social activist during the late 1800s and early 1900s. She fought to change many things. She was against slavery and alcohol. One time, she wanted to speak against alcohol at a meeting. She was not allowed to because she was a woman. This made Anthony mad! After that, Anthony started fighting for women's rights. She wanted women and men to be equal under the law.

But men did not listen to women. How could Anthony get them to listen? She decided to fight for women's suffrage. Suffrage is the right to vote. If women could vote, they could help choose the country's leaders. They could choose leaders that thought men and women should be equal.

Anthony taught others about women's rights. She gave speeches and ran a newspaper about women's rights. She wanted people to join her cause.

In 1872, Anthony even voted! It was still illegal for women to vote though. She was charged a fine. Anthony refused to pay.

In 1878, Anthony presented Congress with an amendment. The amendment would give women the right to vote. It finally became a law in 1920.

Read each question. Circle the right answer.

1. What did Susan B. Anthony fight against?

   a) slavery   **b)** women's rights   **c)** voting

2. *Suffrage* is the right to _____. **a)** own slaves   **b)** vote   **c)** drink alcohol

3. How did Susan B. Anthony teach others about women's rights?

   a) She gave speeches.   **b)** She ran a newspaper.   **c)** both (a) and (b)

4. In what year did women get the right to vote?   **a)** 1872   **b)** 1878   **c)** 1920

Renewable Bamboo!

We use many parts of nature. We use sunlight, water, animals, and plants. Some of these things do not run out. We use sunlight to power a lot of things. There will always be more sunlight. We can use it over and over. This makes sunlight renewable.

Other things in nature do run out. Many hardwood trees grow slowly. It can take 60 years for a new tree to grow! We use trees to build many things. We use them to make paper. We used to cut down trees very quickly. There was not enough time for new ones to grow. Trees were running out. Now we try to reuse cut wood. We recycle our paper.

We try to keep nature healthy. One way is to use only the renewable parts. Plants that grow very quickly are renewable. They will not run out. Bamboo is a renewable plant. Some kinds of bamboo grow two feet in one day!

Bamboo is very useful. It is stronger than many hardwood trees. It can be used to make furniture or floors. It can be used to make toys or bowls. Bamboo can even be used to make clothing. Bamboo fabric is supersoft!

Finish each sentence.

1. We use _____ to power many things.

2. _____ grow slowly.

3. Plants that grow quickly are _____ parts of nature.

4. _____ is stronger than many hardwood trees.

Football or Soccer?

Football is a popular sport in America. To Americans, football is the sport with the odd-shaped brown ball. We think of helmets and lots of padding. We think of tackling and touchdowns. But the word "football" means something different in other countries.

Outside of America, football is the sport with the round black-and-white ball. It means shin guards and cleats. It means kicking and goals. Other countries call it football. We call it soccer. Why?

The two sports started as the same game! It was popular in England in the 1800s. But every team played the game a little differently. It was confusing to play together! In 1863, some clubs wanted to form one game. They tried to make one set of rules. But there were some disagreements. The group split into two groups. There were two different games with two sets of rules. One game was called association football. The other game was called rugby football.

American football grew from the rugby football rules. It became a whole new sport! Soccer grew from association football. The name "soccer" comes from the "S-O-C" in the word "association"!

Read each sentence. Circle *true* or *false*.

1. American football is the same game as football in other countries.	true	false
2. Soccer is the same game as football in other countries.	true	false
3. American football grew from association football.	true	false
4. The name "soccer" came from the name "association football."	true	false

Venus Flytrap

You know that some animals eat plants. But did you know that some plants eat animals? It is true! These plants are carnivores. A carnivore is a meat eater. Most carnivores are animals. But there are some plants that are carnivores too!

Most plant carnivores eat bugs. These plants usually grow in soil that lacks nutrients. They get nutrients from the bugs instead. Plants cannot chase bugs though. They need to trap them. Different plants use different methods to trap bugs. One well-known plant carnivore is the Venus flytrap.

The Venus flytrap uses a snap trap method to catch bugs. It even catches small frogs sometimes! Each trap on the plant has trigger hairs. When a bug passes the trap, it brushes the trigger hairs. This needs to happen two times. Then the trap snaps closed. The bug is stuck inside. The trap stays closed for 10 days. It takes that long to digest the bug. Then the trap opens. It waits for more food. Each trap only catches up to six times. Then it turns brown, withers, and falls off the plant.

Answer the questions below.

1. What is a carnivore?

_____

2. What do most carnivore plants eat?

_____

3. What method does the Venus flytrap use to catch bugs?

_____

4. How long does it take for the Venus flytrap to digest a bug?

_____

Alexander Graham Bell

Alexander Graham Bell was a Scottish inventor. He invented many things throughout his life. He started inventing when he was still a child. His first invention was a wheat husker. This was a machine that removed the husk from wheat grains quickly. Bell was only 12 years old!

Bell's most famous invention is the telephone. His mother and wife were both deaf. He taught deaf students how to speak. Bell studied the human voice. He did experiments with sound. These interests led to his ideas for a telephone.

Bell had an assistant named Thomas Watson. The two men made plans for a telephone. They got a patent for their plans. The patent was an official paper that said no one else could make the same invention. They got it just in time! A man named Elisha Gray was trying to make a telephone too. Bell and Watson kept working. They built a telephone to test. They made some changes. Finally they got it right. On March 10, 1876, Bell talked to Watson on the telephone. And Watson could hear him!

Bell's first telephone looked very different from our phones today. His invention was just the beginning!

What's the order? Write 1, 2, 3, 4 on the lines.

_____ Alexander Graham Bell taught deaf students how to speak.

_____ Alexander Graham Bell made the first successful telephone.

_____ Alexander Graham Bell invented the wheat husker.

_____ Alexander Graham Bell got a patent for the telephone.

The Rubber Tree

We make lots of things from rubber. We make car tires from it. We make rain boots from it. We make pencil erasers from it. Pencil erasers rub out pencil marks. This is why it is called rubber!

Did you know that rubber comes from a tree? It comes from the rubber tree! The liquid in the rubber tree is called latex. Latex lies under the tree's bark. Cut into the bark. Latex flows out! Then it is turned into rubber.

Rubber trees grow in South American rain forests. Native South American tribes made rubber from latex many centuries ago. No one knows exactly when these tribes discovered rubber. But Christopher Columbus knew about rubber! In 1493, he took a second trip to the Americas. Columbus visited Haiti. He saw natives playing with a rubber ball!

There are many different plants that make latex. But we use only the rubber tree to make rubber. Why? Some latex is hard to turn into rubber. This tree's latex is easy to turn into rubber. Also, this tree actually makes more latex when it is cut!

Answer the questions below.

1. Why is rubber called rubber?

_____

2. What is the liquid in a rubber tree called?

_____

3. Where do rubber trees grow?

_____

4. Where did Christopher Columbus first see rubber?

_____

Breakfast Pizza

Do you like pizza? You have probably enjoyed pizza for lunch or dinner. But how about having pizza for breakfast? Try it! This recipe for breakfast pizza is sweet and delicious. You will need:

pizza dough
flour
cream cheese
sliced bananas
berries
honey

With an adult's help, preheat the oven to 350 degrees F (177 degrees C). Roll out your dough on a floured surface. Roll it until it's a large circle. When the oven is ready, have an adult help you put the dough on a baking sheet and transfer it to the oven. Bake it for about 20 minutes. Wait until it's golden brown. Then, remove the cooked pizza dough from the oven. Allow it to cool slightly. Now the fun begins! Spread your crust with cream cheese and honey. Layer fruit however you like. Enjoy!

What's the order? Write 1, 2, 3, 4 on the lines.

_____ Spread cream cheese and honey on the crust.

_____ Enjoy a sweet pizza treat!

_____ Roll out dough in a large circle.

_____ Preheat the oven.

Get Up and Move!

Exercise keeps your body strong. It makes your muscles stronger. It makes your bones stronger. It helps your reflexes and coordination. Imagine someone throws a ball at your head. You can catch the ball. Or you can duck out of the way. With good reflexes and coordination, your body knows what to do quickly. Exercise also makes your heart stronger. This is important! Your heart pumps blood to your whole body. A strong heart does this job better.

Exercise keeps your body healthy. You get fewer diseases, like diabetes. It makes your immune system stronger. You catch fewer colds.

Exercise helps your mind too. Your strong heart pumps more blood to your brain. This makes your brain work better. You can focus more in school. You can get better grades. You can even sleep better. It also helps your mood. Exercise gives you more energy. It helps you feel happier. It helps you stay calmer.

There are lots of ways to get exercise. Play a sport with friends. Have a dance party. Swing on the monkey bars. Ride a bicycle. Just keep moving!

Read each sentence. Circle *true* or *false*.

1. Exercise makes your body strong.	true	false
2. Exercise makes you catch a lot of colds.	true	false
3. Exercise makes it hard to focus in school.	true	false
4. Exercise gives you energy.	true	false

Geysers

Geysers are natural fountains. A geyser is a pool of water that erupts. Water shoots up into the air. It looks like someone turned on a giant fire hose. But it is natural! The water shoots up with a lot of force. Some geysers shoot water just a few feet high. Others shoot up several hundred feet!

Geysers happen in hot springs. Springs are places where water flows up from the ground. Hot springs are often near volcanoes. The volcano's hot magma heats up the water underground. Some hot springs are just hot pools of water. Not all of them are geysers.

Geysers happen when space underground is small. Water tries to squeeze through the small space. Pressure builds. When the water nears the ground, pressure drops. This change in pressure causes the water to shoot up.

There are about 1,000 active geysers in the world. Half of them are in Yellowstone National Park. This is in Wyoming in the United States. Yellowstone National Park's most famous geyser is called Old Faithful. Old Faithful erupts on average every 91 minutes!

Many famous geysers are in Iceland too. They are all over the country. The word "geyser" comes from the Icelandic word "geysir." "Geysir" means "to gush."

Finish each sentence.

1. Geysers are _____ that erupt.

2. Hot _____ from volcanoes heat water underground.

3. Half of the world's geysers are in _____.

4. The word "geyser" comes from the Icelandic word that means

_____.

The Wright Brothers

In the 1800s, most people could not imagine being able to fly. But two brothers could. Their names were Orville and Wilbur Wright.

In 1878, Orville was 7 years old. Wilbur was 11. Their father gave them a flying toy. When they pulled a string, the toy spun into the air. The brothers adored the toy. When it broke, they built their own. Their love of flight began!

As they grew, the Wright brothers' interest in flying grew too. They read about gliders. Gliders are like giant kites. They glide on the wind. But they are big enough to hold a person. The brothers started making their own gliders.

In 1896, the Wright brothers heard about a deadly glider accident. They decided the key to flying was making a machine with an engine. They spent many years making their flying machine. They studied how birds use their wings. They studied how propellers work. They studied different kinds of engines.

Finally, they built the first successful airplane! They tested the airplane in Kitty Hawk, North Carolina, on December 17, 1903. Orville flew for only 12 seconds during the first flight. Still, it was a success!

Answer the questions below.

1. How old were the Wright Brothers when they got their first flying toy?

2. What is a glider?

3. What did the Wright brothers study to design their airplane's wings?

4. How long was the Wright brothers' first flight?

Echolocation

Shout across a canyon or into a well. You will hear your own voice come back to you! That is an echo. Some animals use echoes to find their way. The fancy word for this is "echolocation."

Some bats use echolocation. They hunt for food at night. They cannot see well. They use their hearing instead. Bats make sounds while they fly. The sounds bounce off nearby objects. Then they bounce back to the bats. The bats learn a lot from the sounds that bounce back. They know if there is a rock or a tree in the way. They know if there are bugs nearby. They can tell how near or far these things are. They can even tell if a bug has a hard or soft body!

Dolphins use echolocation too. Dolphins have great eyesight. But in very deep water, there is not a lot of light. It is harder to see. Dolphins send out sounds to find their way.

Some blind people have even learned to use echolocation! They click their tongues or snap their fingers. They listen to the sounds that bounce back. This takes training and practice. But some people use it with success.

Finish each sentence.

1. Some animals use _____ to find their way.

2. _____ bounce off objects. Then they bounce back.

3. Some bats and _____ use echolocation.

4. Blind people can learn to use echolocation. It takes _____ and practice.

Farmers Markets

Today's farmers markets have roots in history. The earliest farmers markets go back 12,000 years! This is when farming first started. Farmers would meet to trade their extra crops. Today's farmers markets are a bit different. Farmers sell their crops directly to shoppers.

Farmers markets are good for farmers. When farmers sell crops to grocery stores, they share the money. When they sell to shoppers, they keep all the money. Also, farmers get to know the shoppers. This is good for business! People start shopping from the same farmers again and again.

Farmers markets are good for shoppers. They can buy healthy food. The food comes from nearby farms. It does not have to travel far. This means it is fresher. It tastes better.

Farmers markets are good for communities. Farmers do not travel far to the markets. This means less air pollution from trucks. Shoppers are likely to stop in other nearby stores too. This is good for the businesses. Farmers markets are a good meeting place for neighbors. They also link people from the country and the city. This gives the farmers and shoppers a sense of community.

Draw a line from each item to a reason farmers markets are good for it.

Farmers	They keep more money from sales.
Shoppers	Local stores do more business.
Communities	They buy fresher food.

Animal Fossils

Press your thumb into some clay. Let the clay dry out and harden. Your thumbprint will stay in the clay. This is kind of like a fossil.

Animals can make fossils. A footprint in mud can turn into a fossil. The mud hardens. Over time, the mud changes into rock. The footprint is still pressed into the rock.

Animals can also turn into fossils after they die. An animal's body may sink in mud. It may be buried by sand. Over time, the soft parts of its body rot. The hard parts like teeth and bones stay. Then the mud or sand hardens. The bones leave a print in the rock.

A footprint fossil is called a trace fossil. Trace fossils show signs of an animal's busy life. Eggshells can turn into trace fossils. So can nests. A bone fossil is called a body fossil. Body fossils show prints of an animal's body. Plants can be body fossils too.

Scientists use fossils to study the past. They use them to learn about changes over time. The prints must be 10,000 years old to be called fossils.

Answer the questions below.

1. What is a body fossil?

_____

2. What does a trace fossil show?

_____

3. Name three examples of trace fossils.

_____

4. How do scientists use fossils?

_____

Holi

Holi is a Hindu holiday. It comes from North India. But people celebrate it all over the world. Holi is in March. It marks the beginning of spring.

Holi honors a Hindu story about a prince named Prahlad. Prahlad prayed to a god named Vishnu. His father did not want Prahlad to pray to any gods. This made the father very angry. He tried to kill Prahlad. But Prahlad did not die. He tried again and again. But Prahlad still did not die. Finally, he made Prahlad sit in the middle of a big bonfire. But Prahlad did not burn! Vishnu had protected him.

Hindus honor this story on the eve before Holi. They light a big bonfire. They think about good winning over evil. It is a happy time!

The next day, Hindus have a big party. There is singing and dancing. Holi is sometimes called the Festival of Colors. This is because everyone throws colored powder and water. People wear old clothes because it gets messy! It is a fun and joyous day. Non-Hindus have even joined the party!

Finish each sentence.

1. Holi is a Hindu holiday from _____ .

2. _____ protected the prince.

3. On the eve before Holi, people light a big _____ .

4. Holi is sometimes called the _____ .

Fireflies

Fireflies are also called lightning bugs. Both names are because the bugs can make their own light. Firefly light can be orange, yellow, or green.

Fireflies hibernate when they are babies. The babies are called larvae. Larvae hibernate during the winter. Some dig into the ground. Others hibernate under tree bark. They come out in the spring. They eat a lot. They change into adult fireflies.

Fireflies live in parks, meadows, and forests. They like wet places. You will not find them in deserts! They live in many places all over the world. But they do not live in Antarctica. Fireflies come out at night. Many people enjoy finding fireflies in their backyards. They are pretty magical!

Firefly larvae use their light to warn predators. The light shows that the larvae are not tasty. It shows that they may be toxic. Adult fireflies use their light for a different reason. Adult fireflies use their lights to find mates. A male flashes his light in a pattern. This lets females know he wants to mate. If a female notices, she flashes her light too. The two fireflies flash their lights until they meet.

Read each question. Circle the right answer.

1. What is another name for fireflies?

   a) larvae   **b)** lightning bugs   **c)** predators

2. Where do firefly larvae hibernate?

   a) in the ground   **b)** in tree bark   **c)** both (a) and (b)

3. Where do fireflies live?   **a)** deserts   **b)** Antarctica   **c)** meadows

4. Why do firefly larvae use their light?

   a) to warn predators   **b)** to find mates   **c)** to make a magical show

The National Archives

Archives are like libraries of history. In an archive there are paper records and photographs. There are sound recordings and videos. There are diaries and scrapbooks. There are old cameras and computers.

Libraries have printed books and magazines. There are many more copies of these materials. You can find them in other libraries and in stores. Objects in an archive are less common. Many of them are one of a kind.

Objects in an archive keep a record of history. A university archive tells the history of that school. A business archive tells the history of that company. A film archive tells the history of movies.

Our government has its own archives! The National Archives stores records from our country's history. The main archives are in Washington, DC, and Maryland. There are smaller archives all over the country. The National Archives keeps records from our presidents. They keep records from our military. They even keep original documents from our Founding Fathers! The records in the National Archives are public. Anyone can ask to see them. Many are ready to view on the Internet. You can view them online at www.archives.gov/.

Read each sentence. Circle *true* or *false*.

1. Archives and libraries are the same thing.　　true　　false

2. Archives store common printed books and magazines.　　true　　false

3. The National Archives keeps a record of US history.　　true　　false

4. Only the president can see records from the National Archives.　　true　　false

Shadows and Sundials

Your shadow follows you on a sunny day. But it is never in the same place. It is never the same length. Why does it change?

Sunlight cannot pass through your body. Your body blocks the light. The result is your shadow. The sun moves in the sky. As it moves, your shadow changes. When the sun is behind you, your shadow is in front. When the sun is in front of you, your shadow is behind. When the sun is high up, your shadow is short. When the sun is low, your shadow is long.

People did not always have clocks. They used the position of the sun to tell time. They used shadows too. People used shadows to tell time as early as 3500 BCE. They used a gnomon. A gnomon was a vertical pole. The pole made a shadow on sunny days. People knew the time of day from how long the shadow was.

Around 1500 BCE, Egyptians made the first sundials. Sundials look a bit like clocks. Different lines mark different hours. A gnomon in the center casts a shadow around the sundial. As the sun moves throughout the day, the shadow points to a different hour.

Answer the questions below.

1. Why does your body make a shadow on sunny days?

_____

2. Where is the sun when your shadow is long?

_____

3. When did Egyptians make the first sundials?

_____

4. What do the lines on a sundial mark?

_____

Helen Keller

Helen Keller was born in 1880. She was a very smart baby. She started talking at 6 months old! At 19 months old, Keller got very sick. She probably had scarlet fever. No one knows for sure. In those days, scarlet fever could be deadly. Keller was lucky to live. But the sickness made her blind and deaf.

Keller could not see or hear. She started making up signs. She used them to tell others what she wanted. Still, it was hard to communicate. Keller was very frustrated. She threw a lot of tantrums.

Her parents were fed up. In 1887, they hired Anne Sullivan to teach their daughter. Sullivan used sign language letters to spell. She spelled words into Keller's hands. After a month, Keller started to understand!

Keller learned to read Braille. She learned to write. She learned to talk. Keller graduated from college. She wrote magazine articles. She wrote many books too. Keller traveled the world. She gave speeches about blindness and deafness. She raised money to help other blind and deaf people. Keller proved that being blind and deaf does not have to limit what you can do.

Finish each sentence.

1. Being sick made Helen Keller _____ and _____ .

2. _____ taught Helen Keller to spell words with sign language.

3. Helen Keller wrote books and _____ .

4. Helen Keller _____ to help other blind and deaf people.

Wind Power

People have used wind power for thousands of years. There were boats powered by wind back in 5000 BCE! By 200 BCE, people started using simple windmills. They used windmills to pump water. They used windmills to grind grains.

Today, we use wind to make electricity. Wind turbines look like giant fans. They stand outside in open fields. Wind turns the turbine's blades. The blades turn parts inside the turbine. These parts produce electricity. This electricity can power a building. Often, wind turbines are connected to a power grid. The electricity spreads across a larger area.

Many power companies build wind farms. Wind farms are areas with many wind turbines. Together, the wind turbines produce more electricity. Some wind farms only have a few wind turbines. Some have several hundred! Some wind farms are offshore. The wind turbines stand in water. It is often very windy over water.

Wind farms produce clean energy. They do not pollute our world. They also produce renewable energy. Wind cannot run out. We can always use more wind to make more electricity.

Read each sentence. Circle *true* or *false*.

1. Wind turbines turn wind into electricity.	true	false
2. All wind farms are offshore in the water.	true	false
3. Wind farms make a lot of pollution.	true	false
4. Wind is renewable energy because it cannot run out.	true	false

Aztec Ruins National Monument

Ruins are groups of deserted buildings. No one lives in them. No one keeps them in good shape. Over time, they fall apart. Ruins teach us about the people who used to live there.

The Aztec Ruins National Monument is in New Mexico in the United States. In the mid-1800s, settlers came to the area. They saw the ruins. They thought people from Mexico's Aztec tribe built them. But they were wrong! The Native Americans that lived in the buildings were from the Pueblo tribe.

Pueblo people started building the site that became Aztec Ruins around the year 1110. They lived there for about 200 years. In the late 1200s, the area had a drought. There was very little rain. The Pueblo people could not farm. By 1300, they left the area. They needed to find wetter land. The buildings slowly fell apart.

The Pueblo people built several great houses. These were multi-story buildings. Some had more than 400 rooms! Visitors to Aztec Ruins can see remains of these buildings. They can learn about the Pueblo people from hundreds of years ago.

Read each question. Circle the right answer.

1. What are ruins?   **a)** deserted buildings
   b) buildings that are falling apart   **c)** both (a) and (b)

2. Where is the Aztec Ruins National Monument?
   a) in New Mexico   **b)** in Mexico   **c)** in Pueblo

3. Who lived at the Aztec Ruins?   **a)** people from the Pueblo tribe
   b) people from the Aztec tribe   **c)** settlers

4. What was a great house?   **a)** a monument
   b) a multistory building   **c)** a building used for ceremonies

The Amazon Rain Forest

Rain forests are forests that get a lot of rain. It can rain more than one inch every day! There are tropical rain forests all over the world. They are found near the equator. They are very warm.

The biggest rain forest is the Amazon in South America. It is about the size of the 48 connected states in the United States! The Amazon is in South America. More than half of the rain forest is in Brazil. The rest spreads across eight other countries.

Many plants and animals live in the Amazon. There are more kinds of plants and animals there than anywhere in the world! The biggest mix of plants and animals live in the canopy. The canopy is a thick coat of trees. The canopy blocks most of the sunlight. The rain forest floor is very dark.

People live in the Amazon too. There are more than 400 different native tribes! Native people used to stay in the rain forest. They found food and shelter there. They made medicine from plants. Now they sometimes leave. They go into nearby towns to sell food. They use human-made pots and pans.

Answer the questions below.

1. What is a rain forest?

_____

2. What is the biggest rain forest in the world?

_____

3. How many countries does the Amazon spread across?

_____

4. What is the Amazon's canopy?

_____

Rosa Parks

Rosa Parks was born in Alabama in 1913. She grew up in a segregated time and place. People of different races could not mix. They could not go to school together. They could not drink from the same water fountains. They could not sit next to each other on buses. This bothered Parks even as a child.

When she grew up, Parks worked as a housekeeper and seamstress. But she had bigger plans. Parks wanted African Americans to have equal rights. She fought to end segregation. She worked to get the courts to change segregation laws.

On December 1, 1955, Parks took a stand. She was riding a city bus in Montgomery, Alabama, in the United States. The bus was full. A white man wanted a seat. The bus driver told Parks to give up her seat. But Parks refused! She was arrested and sent to jail.

Other African-Americans were very upset. They started a boycott of the Montgomery buses. They refused to ride the buses. The boycott lasted for 381 days. Without African-American riders, the buses lost a lot of money. Finally, the law was changed. All people could sit wherever they wanted on the buses.

Finish each sentence.

1. Rosa Parks grew up in a _____ time and place.

2. _____ could not go to school together.

3. Rosa Parks worked to get the _____ to change segregation laws.

4. Rosa Parks refused to _____ on a bus.

Ultraviolet Light

The sun gives off a lot of light. Some of it is ultraviolet light. It is called UV light for short. Some animals can see UV light. But people cannot see it! Scientists use special tools to measure UV light. They use special cameras to take pictures of it.

Some sunlight is good for us. Our skin uses the UV light to make vitamin D. Vitamin D is important for our bodies! It helps make our bones strong.

But too much UV light is not good for us. It causes painful sunburns. It ages our skin. It can lead to skin cancer. UV light can also harm our eyes.

Earth's air helps protect us from the sun's UV light. There are gases in the air around Earth. The gases block a lot of the UV light. It cannot pass through to Earth. One of these gases is called ozone.

There is less ozone in Earth's air than there used to be. It has been decreasing since at least 1985. More UV light passes through to Earth. It is extra important to protect our skin from the sun! We can wear sunscreen. We can wear sunglasses. We can wear hats with wide brims.

Read each sentence. Circle *true* or *false*.

	true	false
1. People can see ultraviolet light.	true	false
2. UV light helps our skin make vitamin D.	true	false
3. Too much UV light causes sunburns.	true	false
4. Ozone blocks all UV light from reaching Earth.	true	false

The Melting Pot

People sometimes call America a melting pot. It is like when we mix different ingredients together in a pot to make a soup. We put chicken, carrots, noodles, and broth in a pot. When the ingredients mix together, they become something new. They are no longer separate ingredients. They mix together to become soup.

Instead of mixed ingredients, America has mixed people. There are many different kinds of people in America. There are people from many different countries. There are people from many different races. They all mix together to make one country.

People from all over the world come to live in America. They are called immigrants. Immigrants bring their cultures with them to America. They bring their ways of living. They bring their beliefs. Over time, they also take in American ways of living. They take in American beliefs. Immigrant cultures change America. American culture changes immigrants. The two mix together.

Some believe that the mix of people and cultures makes America stronger. This is why they call America a melting pot.

Finish each sentence.

1. Some people call America a _____ .

2. _____ from all over the world move to America to live.

3. Immigrants bring their _____ to America.

4. Some people believe that the mix of different people makes America _____ .

Talking Apes

Did you know that some great apes can talk with people? They cannot use their voices. But they can use sign language! Chimpanzees, bonobos, gorillas, and orangutans can all learn sign language.

The first great ape to learn sign language was a chimpanzee named Washoe. Washoe's mother died when she was a baby. She was captured from the wild in 1966. Two scientists raised her like a human child. They planned to teach her sign language. It worked! Washoe learned about 130 signs. She died in 2007. But she showed scientists that apes could understand language.

Koko is a gorilla. She knows sign language too. Koko knows more than 1,000 signs! She even understands when people speak. She can understand about 2,000 spoken words. She makes sentences with three to six signs. Koko has learned more language than any other ape so far.

Washoe and Koko are just two apes that can use sign language. There are many others that have learned sign language too. Great apes are very smart!

Answer the questions below.

1. Name four kinds of great apes that can use sign language.

_____

2. Who was the first great ape to learn sign language?

_____

3. How many signs did Washoe learn?

_____

4. Who is Koko?

_____

The Dust Bowl

In the late 1800s, many people settled in the Great Plains. This is an area in the middle of the United States. There is a lot of open, flat land. There was a lot of grass on the land. The settlers got rid of it. They plowed the land to make farms. The settlers did not know much about farming. They plowed the land too much.

In 1931, a drought hit the Great Plains. This means there was very little rain. The land got very dry. Farmers had a hard time growing crops. The drought lasted for eight years!

There was no grass to hold the dry soil in place. The soil turned into dust. The dust blew into the air. There were many dust storms during this time. The area became known as the dust bowl. The dust bowl covered parts of Oklahoma, Texas, Kansas, Colorado, and New Mexico. One storm even reached all the way to the Atlantic Ocean!

Farmers could not grow crops. They had no money. The storms destroyed many homes. Farmers had to leave their farms. Many moved west to look for work. Others died from breathing in too much dust. The drought finally ended in 1939.

What's the order? Write 1, 2, 3, 4 on the lines.

_____ People settled in the Great Plains.

_____ Dust storms blew through the air.

_____ Settlers plowed the land too much.

_____ An eight-year drought hit the Great Plains.

Pushing and Pulling

Objects cannot move by themselves. Forces need to move them. Forces can change how fast the object moves. They can also change the direction the object is going.

There are two main kinds of forces. There is pushing. There is pulling. When you push or pull an object, you are applying force to it.

Pushing an object moves it away from the force. Push your friend on a swing. You are the force. Your friend is the object. Pushing the swing moves it away from you.

Pulling an object moves it toward the force. Pull a toy wagon. You are the force. The wagon is the object. Pulling the wagon moves it toward you.

The size of the force changes how much the object moves. Kick a ball. Kicking is a pushing force. A small kick makes the ball roll slowly. It moves just a short length. A big kick makes the ball roll fast. It moves much farther away.

Gravity is a force in nature. It is a pulling force. Jump up in the air. You will naturally fall back down to the ground. That is gravity pulling you down!

Finish each sentence.

1. Objects need _____ to move them.

2. Two kinds of forces are _____ and _____ .

3. Pulling an object moves it _____ the force.

4. _____ is a pulling force in nature.

Creating an Oral History

We often learn history from textbooks. Sometimes the words in the books feel flat. It is hard to imagine that what we read really happened.

Oral histories are spoken records about the past. The word "oral" means "spoken." An oral history zeroes in on a certain time or event. Historians interview people who lived during that time. They ask about what the people did. They ask them how they felt. Oral histories make the past seem more real.

You can be a historian. You can make an oral history! First decide on your subject. Then prepare a list of questions about the subject. Next find people to interview. Maybe you want to learn about how your school has changed. You can interview some teachers who have worked there for a long time. Maybe you want to know what life was like when your parents were children. You can interview your parents and your friends' parents. Be sure to record your interviews! Use a tape recorder or a video camera. This way you have a lasting record.

Answer the questions below. Use the information from your interviews to create an outline for your oral history.

1. Whom did you interview? _____

_____

2. What questions did you ask? _____

_____

3. What did you learn? _____

_____

4. What would you include in your oral history? _____

_____

Earthquakes

Have you ever felt the ground shake under your feet? You may have lived through an earthquake! Earthquakes can happen all over the world. But there are certain places where they happen most often.

The surface of Earth is not one whole piece. It is broken into many pieces. These pieces are called plates. The plates fit together like a puzzle to cover Earth. The plates are always moving. The movement is very slow. The plates move only half an inch to almost four inches (1–10 cm) each year. Sometimes they move away from each other. Sometimes they bump into each other. Sometimes they slide under each other.

The borders between plates are made from many faults. Faults are cracks in the surface of Earth. Faults have rough edges. Sometimes fault edges get stuck on each other. But the rest of the plate or plates keep moving. When the faults finally unstick, the land shakes. This is an earthquake!

Earthquakes range in size. Some earthquakes are huge. They destroy buildings and kill people. Depending where earthquakes are, they can cause mudslides or tsunamis. Others are very small. People might not even feel them at all!

Finish each sentence.

1. The surface of Earth is broken into pieces called _____ .

2. Earth's plates move _____ each year.

3. _____ are cracks in Earth's surface.

4. Fault edges sometimes stick on each other because they are _____ .

The Internet

People all over the world use the Internet. It is hard to imagine life without it! But we did not always have the Internet. The Internet became available for anyone to use in the 1990s. Most people did not even have computers at home until the late 1990s. Daily life changed quickly after that.

Before the Internet, most people didn't have access to e-mail. If your friend lived far away, you wrote letters on paper. You mailed the letter in the regular mail. It took a few days to reach your friend's mailbox. Now we write e-mail more than letters. It takes a few seconds for an e-mail to reach your friend's inbox.

Before the Internet, there was no online shopping. You went to a store to shop for most things. Sometimes you ordered things from a mail-order catalog. Now we visit Web sites to shop in online stores. We can buy almost anything on the Internet! We can buy clothing. We can buy books and toys. We can even buy groceries!

We use the Internet for so much more too. We check the weather on the Internet. We check movie times. We even read the newspaper on the Internet!

Answer the questions below.

1. When did it become common to have computers at home?

_____

2. How did people write to their friends before there was e-mail?

_____

3. How did people shop before there were online stores?

_____

4. Name three uses of the Internet besides e-mail and shopping.

_____

Scuba Diving

How can we learn about life in the deep sea? We can go deep sea diving! It is called scuba diving. SCUBA is an acronym. Each letter stands for a word. SCUBA stands for **s**elf-**c**ontained **u**nderwater **b**reathing **a**pparatus. When you dive, you wear special scuba gear. The gear lets you breathe underwater. You wear a mask on your face. You wear an oxygen tank on your back. The mask and the tank are connected. You can breathe oxygen straight from the tank.

Not just anyone can go scuba diving! First you must pass a health test. Then you must take classes. It is important to be specially trained.

A French man invented modern scuba gear. His name was Jacques Cousteau. He tested the gear in 1943. Cousteau fell in love with diving!

Cousteau started selling his gear in 1946. By the 1950s, scuba diving became more popular. In 1968, Cousteau started a television show. It was called *The Undersea World of Jacques Cousteau*. He brought cameras underwater. More people wanted to dive. Today, almost one million people are trained to scuba dive each year!

Answer the questions below.

1. What do the letters stand for in SCUBA?

_____

2. Name some important scuba gear.

_____

3. What are some steps you must take before you can scuba dive?

_____

4. Who invented modern scuba gear?

_____

Amelia Earhart

Amelia Earhart grew up in the early 1900s. Back then, women did not have equal rights to men. But that did not bother Earhart. She became a pilot! There were only a few women pilots in those days. Flying was not as safe as it is now. Earhart did not care. She was bold. She liked daring adventures.

In December 1920, Earhart went on her first airplane ride. The ride was only 10 minutes long. But Earhart knew right away that she loved it. She decided that she wanted to learn to fly. In January 1921, Earhart started flying lessons. A few months later, she bought her first airplane.

Earhart was the first woman pilot to do many things. She flew across the Atlantic Ocean by herself. She flew across the entire United States without stopping. She broke record after record!

In 1935, Earhart decided on her biggest adventure. She wanted to fly all the way around the world! She got a new airplane for the trip. She found a partner to fly with her. She started the big trip in June 1937. One month later, she disappeared. She had been flying over the Pacific Ocean. No one has ever found her.

Read each sentence. Circle *true* or *false*.

	true	false
1. Amelia Earhart was very fearful.	true	false
2. Amelia Earhart learned to fly in December 1920.	true	false
3. Amelia Earhart bought her first airplane in 1921.	true	false
4. Amelia Earhart broke many flying records.	true	false

Organic Farming

Farmers started to use human-made chemicals in the 1940s. Today, many farms still use chemicals. These farms add chemicals to the ground. This makes the soil richer. They spray chemicals on their crops. This kills weeds. It keeps pests away. They feed animals chemicals. This makes the animals grow bigger. It makes them produce more milk or eggs. Farms can grow more. They can sell more. It is good for business. But it means that we eat those chemicals! A lot of our food comes from these farms.

Organic farmers do not use chemicals. In the 1960s–70s, keeping Earth healthy became important to people. Organic farming grew popular again. Today, more people know about organic farms. They are even more popular.

Organic farmers use natural ways to feed the soil. For example, cow dung makes soil richer. They use natural ways to keep pests away. For example, they put special nets over the crops. They feed animals only what they would eat in nature. Food from organic farms does not have chemicals in it.

Finish each sentence.

1. In the 1940s, farmers started to use _____ .

2. Spraying crops with chemicals keeps _____ away.

3. Feeding animals chemicals makes them grow _____ .

4. _____ farmers do not use chemicals.

Graffiti vs. Art

There is a lot of art in outdoor spaces. Murals cover outside walls. Sculptures stand in parks and plazas. People come to see this art. They value this art. They think it makes neighborhoods and parks more beautiful. Often, the same people get angry about graffiti. They do not like seeing graffiti. Why?

Murals and sculptures are commissioned works of art. This means the artists are paid to make the art. A business pays an artist to paint a mural. A city government pays an artist to build a sculpture. The people who own the property want the art to be there.

Graffiti artists paint in outdoor spaces too. They paint on walls. They paint on trains. They paint on traffic signs. But no one paid them. They do not have permission to paint. Graffiti is a crime. It is illegal to ruin someone else's property.

Some graffiti artists are very talented. Their art is very beautiful. Often they want more people to enjoy their art. They paint in public so that lots of people can see it. It is still illegal! But sometimes people do enjoy their art a lot. Sometimes people then hire the artist to paint.

Read each sentence. Circle *true* or *false*.

1. Commissioned art is illegal.	true	false
2. Graffiti is when the artist is paid to make art.	true	false
3. Graffiti is a crime.	true	false
4. Sometimes graffiti artists get hired to paint.	true	false

Egyptian Pyramids

The Egyptian pyramids are ancient buildings in Egypt. They are shaped like pyramids. Egyptians built them thousands of years ago. The pyramids are tombs. Tombs are resting places for people after they die. These tombs were built for pharaohs. Pharaohs were rulers in ancient Egypt.

After they died, pharaohs were made into mummies. Ancient Egyptians believed this would let the pharaoh live forever. They buried the mummies in the pyramids. They buried them with their belongings. They buried them with some riches. Over time, robbers took these things from most of the pyramids.

There are more than 130 pyramids. The Great Pyramid of Giza is the most famous one. It was built for a pharaoh named Khufu. It was built around 2550 BCE. It took many years to finish it. The Great Pyramid is the biggest Egyptian pyramid. When it was new, it was 481 feet (146.6 m) tall! That is more than 44 stories high. Now it is about 30 feet (9.1 m) shorter. The top capstone is missing. The stone underneath has worn away.

People travel to see the Egyptian pyramids. They come from all over the world. Millions of travelers visit the pyramids each year!

Answer the questions below.

1. What is a tomb?

_____

2. What was a pharaoh?

_____

3. Why did ancient Egyptians turn pharaohs into mummies after they died?

_____

4. Which is the most famous Egyptian pyramid?

_____

Oil Spills

Oil spills are messy. They pollute Earth. They kill animals.

Sometimes oil spills happen on purpose. The people who spill the oil might not know it is bad. They might know that it is bad and do it anyway. Sometimes this happens during wars. Most oil spills are accidents though.

Oil spills can happen on land. Sometimes oil trucks tip over on the highway. Oil spills out. It covers the road and the nearby grass. These are easier to clean up.

They can happen in the water too. Sometimes oil ships crash into rocks. The rocks tear into the ship's oil tank. Oil leaks out. It floats on the water and covers animals. These are hard to clean up. They take a lot of time and cost a lot of money to clean up.

Birds try to clean the oil from their feathers. They end up eating some of the oil. It poisons them. Seals trap air in their fur for warmth. When their fur has oil on it, they can't trap this air. Their temperature drops. Whales come out of the water to breathe. Oil clogs their blowholes. Oil spills also destroy algae and seaweed too.

Read each sentence. Circle *true* or *false*.

	true	false
1. Most oil spills happen on purpose.	true	false
2. Oil spills happen only in the water.	true	false
3. Oil spills in the water are easy to clean up.	true	false
4. Oil spills harm animals.	true	false

Mardi Gras

Mardi Gras is a Christian holiday. It falls in February or March. It is the day before Ash Wednesday. Some Christians fast on Ash Wednesday. They eat only one full meal that day. Ash Wednesday is the beginning of Lent. During Lent, Some Christians continue to fast for 40 days. Some may also give up a favorite food or activity for those 40 days. "Mardi Gras" means "Fat Tuesday" in French. It is the last chance to eat a lot before the fast begins.

Mardi Gras started in Rome, Italy. The holiday spread through Europe. In 1699, it came to the United States. Louisiana was under French rule at that time. Some French explorers arrived in Louisiana. They landed near today's city of New Orleans. On March 3, 1699, the explorers had a small party for Mardi Gras. It was the first American Mardi Gras!

Today, lots of people celebrate Mardi Gras in the United States. It is not just a Christian holiday. The biggest American Mardi Gras party is in New Orleans, Louisiana. People dress up in fancy costumes. They wear masks or makeup. They throw beads. There is a big parade with big floats. There is music and dancing in the streets. It is a very colorful holiday!

Finish each sentence.

1. "Mardi Gras" means _____ in French.

2. Mardi Gras is the last chance to _____ before Ash Wednesday and Lent.

3. _____ brought Mardi Gras to the United States.

4. The biggest Mardi Gras party in the United States is in

_____ .

The Cacao Tree

Did you know chocolate grows on trees? But you will not find a candy bar hanging from a tree. Chocolate is made from part of the cacao tree.

Cacao trees grow in very hot places. They need a lot of rain. They first grew in South America. Now they are common in Central America and Africa too.

Big pods grow on cacao trees. Some pods grow as big as footballs! Each pod has about 50–60 seeds inside. The seeds taste very bitter. No animals will eat them. But people figured out a way to use them.

It takes many steps to turn the seeds into chocolate. The seeds are fermented and dried. They are roasted. The shells are removed. They are ground into a powder. Cocoa powder is used to make chocolate. It is mixed with other things like sugar and milk.

Native tribes in South America used cacao seeds first. The Olmecs discovered cacao more than 3,000 years ago. They figured out how to make cocoa powder. Then they made a kind of hot chocolate drink.

Hernán Cortés was a Spanish explorer. He tasted a chocolate drink with the Aztec tribe. He brought it back to Spain in 1528.

Read each question. Circle the right answer.

1. Where did cacao trees grow first?

   a) Africa
   b) South America
   c) Central America

2. What is inside the cacao pods? a) cocoa powder b) cacao seeds c) footballs

3. What is the first step to turn cacao seeds into cocoa powder?

   a) fermenting
   b) roasting
   c) grinding

4. Who were the first people to use cacao?

   a) the Aztecs
   b) the Spanish
   c) the Olmecs

Navajo Code Talkers

During wars, militaries need to keep secrets. They do not want their enemies to know their plans. How can militaries send secret messages to each other? They use codes!

During World War II, Americans had trouble keeping secrets. The Japanese kept breaking their codes! The Americans needed a new code. They needed one that was very hard to break. One man had an idea for the military. He thought they should use the Navajo language! The Navajo are a Native American tribe. There was no way to write their language. There were no dictionaries to help the enemies understand the words. Navajo words are hard to say. Many words have many different meanings. The Navajo language is hard to learn!

The American military hired Navajos as code talkers. The code talkers made a code. They changed English words. Then they changed them to Navajo. The Navajo word for eggs meant bombs. They also used Navajo words to spell out English words. The Navajo word for ant meant the letter A.

The Navajo code talkers were a big help to America. The Japanese never broke the Navajo code! It helped America win over its enemies.

Answer the questions below.

1. Why do militaries need to keep secrets during war?

_____

2. Who kept breaking the American codes during World War II?

_____

3. What Native American tribe did the American military hire to make a code?

_____

4. Name three reasons Navajo is a hard language to learn.

_____

_____

Camels in Deserts

Deserts are hard places to live. Camels live well in deserts. Their bodies have changed to make it easier to live there.

Camels have thick fur. It protects them from the hot sun. It also keeps them warm at night. Camels have long eyelashes. The lashes block sand from blowing into their eyes. They can close their nostrils. This blocks sand from blowing into their noses.

Camel feet are made for walking in deserts. Their feet spread flat and wide. This keeps them from sinking into the sand. Camel feet have leathery pads on the bottoms. This protects their feet from the hot sand. Camels also have leathery patches on their knees. This lets them kneel in the hot sand.

Camels eat plants. They get water from the plants. Their mouths are leathery. This lets them eat thorny desert plants. Camels can eat cacti! Camels can go for a long time without food or water. They have humps on their backs. The humps are full of fat. They use the fat in their humps for energy. They change the fat into water too. This is why they can go a long time without eating or drinking.

Draw a line from each body part to its purpose.

long eyelashes	store energy
wide feet	protect from hot sand
pads on knees	block blowing sand
leathery mouths	keep from sinking into sand
fatty humps	protect from thorny plants

Jackie Robinson

Jackie Robinson was born in 1919. He loved to play sports. And he was good! In college, Robinson played baseball, basketball, football, and track. He shined in all four sports.

In 1945, Robinson started playing professional baseball. He played in the Negro Leagues. The Negro Leagues were for African-American players.

Branch Rickey was the general manager of the Brooklyn Dodgers. The Brooklyn Dodgers were a team in the major leagues. Rickey saw Robinson play in the Negro Leagues. He offered Robinson a spot on the Dodgers!

Robinson played his first game with the Dodgers in 1947. He was the first African-American player in the major leagues since the late 1800s! Robinson had a tough job. A lot of people did not like that he was African-American. They did not want him in the major leagues. He was treated badly by a lot of people.

Robinson played 10 seasons in the major leagues. He was in the World Series six times. He changed Major League Baseball forever! Today there are many African-American players in the major leagues.

Answer the questions below.

1. What sports did Jackie Robinson play in college?

_____

2. When did Jackie Robinson start playing professional baseball?

_____

3. What were the Negro Leagues?

_____

4. What was special about Jackie Robinson playing in the major leagues?

_____

The First Thanksgiving

In 1620, a group of settlers left Plymouth, England. They wanted to move to new land. They rode on a ship called the *Mayflower*. The settlers landed in America that fall. They started building their new settlement. They called their settlement Plymouth Colony. It was on land that is now part of Massachusetts.

The settlers prepared for winter. They lived on the *Mayflower* and built houses on land. They moved onto land in late January. They gathered whatever supplies they could find. They stole some supplies from nearby Native Americans. This made the Native Americans very angry.

One Native American knew how to speak English. His name was Squanto. Squanto helped the settlers and the Native Americans make peace. He also helped the settlers learn how to survive. He taught them to plant corn. He taught them how to fish.

The first Thanksgiving followed in the fall of 1621. It was a harvest festival. The settlers and the Native Americans joined together. They gathered the food they had planted. They were very thankful for the feast. But they did not call it Thanksgiving until years later.

Finish each sentence.

1. The settlers rode to America on _____ .

2. The settlers called their settlement _____ .

3. _____ helped the settlers learn how to survive.

4. The settlers and the Native Americans were thankful for the food they had planted. The first Thanksgiving was a _____ .

Answer Key

Page 4
1. true
2. true
3. false
4. false

Page 5
1. outer space
2. Russia
3. Neil Armstrong
4. footprints

Page 6
1. a
2. b
3. c
4. b

Page 7
1. true
2. false
3. true
4. false

Page 8
1. a glass jar with a wide opening
2. to drain extra water
3. to filter the water
4. No. It is best to choose plants that need the same kind of environment.

Page 9
1. Independence Day
2. Britain
3. independence; freedom
4. fireworks

Page 10

touch —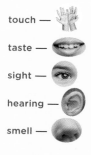

taste —

sight —

hearing —

smell —

Page 11
1. c
2. b
3. c
4. a

Page 12
1. horseback
2. Missouri
3. weather; terrain
4. transcontinental telegraph

Page 13
1. false
2. true
3. false
4. false

Page 14
3
2
4
1

Page 15
1. the solar system
2. center
3. the sun moved around Earth
4. eight

Page 16
1. b
2. b
3. b
4. c

Page 17
1. true
2. false
3. true
4. true

Page 18
1. lava
2. the Pacific Ocean
3. Hawaii
4. Soil near volcanoes is very fertile.

Page 19
1. true
2. true
3. false
4. true

Page 20
1. a
2. c
3. c
4. b

Page 21
1. balance
2. run; kick predators
3. hide
4. adult chickens

Page 22
1. Missouri
2. a team of more than 30 men and supplies
3. almost two and a half years
4. She showed them which plants were safe to eat; she helped them talk to Native Americans.

Page 23
1. false
2. true
3. false
4. false

Page 24
full moon: circle
crescent moon: smile
quarter moon: semicircle
new moon: no light

Page 25
1. California
2. forty-niners
3. Boomtowns
4. ghost towns

Page 26
1. the queen
2. female
3. the worker ants
4. to mate with the queen

Page 27
1. b
2. a
3. c
4. c

Page 28
1
4
2
3

Page 29
1. Senator Gaylord Nelson
2. Americans
3. pollution; energy
4. litter

Page 30
1. candles
2. It picked up sparks from the lightning.
3. It is electricity.
4. the lightning rod

Page 31
1. true
2. true
3. false
4. false

Page 32
1. national
2. stars
3. revolution and freedom
4. 50

Page 33
1. false
2. true
3. false
4. false

Page 34
1. No one can change the land in a national park; it is all natural.
2. a country's government
3. Yes, people are allowed to enjoy national parks.
4. in Wyoming

Page 35
1. germs
2. grandchildren
3. Food banks
4. love; attention

Page 36
1. c
2. b
3. c
4. a

Page 37
1. north
2. poles
3. pull toward
4. north

Page 38
1. true
2. false
3. true
4. false

Page 39
1. c
2. b
3. b
4. a

Page 40
1. It could take six months.
2. Because the railroad was built on Native American land.
3. May 10, 1869
4. one week

Page 41
3
1
4
2

Page 42
lever—seesaw
inclined plane—dump truck
screw—jar lid
wedge—doorstop
wheel and axle—doorknob
pulley—flagpole

Page 43
1. Sharks and remoras help each other.
2. suckerfish
3. Sharks protect remoras from predators. Remoras also eat the shark's leftover food.
4. Remoras eat parasites from the sharks' skin and teeth.

Page 44
1. true
2. false
3. false
4. true

Page 45
4
2
3
1

Page 46
1. true
2. false
3. false
4. true

Page 47
1. mammals
2. paddle
3. stingers
4. dinosaurs

Page 48
1. He wanted African Americans to feel proud of their roots.
2. They build up family, community, and culture.
3. red, black, and green
4. karamu

Page 49
1. true
2. false
3. true
4. false

Page 50
1. freedom and democracy
2. Frédéric-Auguste Bartholdi
3. on Liberty Island in the New York Harbor
4. 354 steps to the top

Page 51
Answers will vary but may include:
1. Changing weather patterns may endanger animals.
2. Too much hunting endangers animals.
3. An animal is extinct.
4. The government works to protect endangered animals.

Page 52
1. a
2. b
3. c
4. c

Page 53
1. sunlight
2. Hardwood trees
3. renewable
4. Bamboo

Page 54
1. false
2. true
3. false
4. true

Page 55
1. a meat eater
2. bugs
3. a snap trap
4. ten days

Page 56
2
4
1
3

Page 57
1. because rubber pencil erasers rub out pencil marks
2. latex
3. South American rain forests
4. Haiti

Page 58
3
4
2
1

Page 59
1. true
2. false
3. false
4. true

Page 60
1. pools of water
2. magma
3. Yellowstone National Park
4. to gush

Page 61
1. Orville was 7 years old. Wilbur was 11 years old.
2. Gliders are like giant kites that glide on the wind.
3. They studied how birds use their wings.
4. The first flight lasted 12 seconds.

Page 62
1. echoes; echolocation
2. Sounds
3. dolphins
4. training

Page 63
Farmers—They keep more money from sales.
Shoppers—They buy fresher food.
Communities—Local stores do more business.

Page 64
1. It is a print of a plant or an animal's body in rock.
2. It shows signs of an animal's busy life.
3. footprints, eggshells, nests
4. They use fossils to study the past and learn about changes over time.

Page 65
1. North India
2. Vishnu
3. bonfire
4. Festival of Colors

Page 66
1. b
2. c
3. c
4. a

Page 67
1. false
2. false
3. true
4. false

Page 68
1. because your body blocks the sunlight
2. It is low in the sky.
3. around 1500 BCE
4. They mark different hours.

Page 69
1. blind; deaf
2. Anne Sullivan
3. magazine articles
4. raised money

Page 70
1. true
2. false
3. false
4. true

Page 71
1. c
2. a
3. a
4. b

Page 72
1. a forest with a lot of rain
2. the Amazon rain forest
3. nine countries
4. a thick coat of branches and leaves

Page 73
1. segregated
2. People of different races
3. courts
4. give up her seat

Page 74
1. false
2. true
3. true
4. false

Page 75
1. melting pot
2. Immigrants
3. cultures; ways of living; beliefs
4. stronger

Page 76
1. chimpanzees, bonobos, gorillas, and orangutans
2. a chimpanzee named Washoe
3. about 130
4. a gorilla that knows sign language

Page 77
1
4
2
3

Page 78
1. forces
2. pushing; pulling
3. toward
4. Gravity

Page 79
Answers will vary.

Page 80
1. plates
2. .5–4 inches (1–10 cm)
3. Faults
4. rough

Page 81
1. the late 1990s
2. They wrote letters on paper and sent them in the regular mail.
3. They ordered from a mail-order catalog.
4. Answers will vary but may include: checking weather; checking movie times; reading the newspaper

Page 82
1. self-contained underwater breathing apparatus
2. mask and oxygen tank
3. pass a health test and get trained in special classes
4. Jacques Cousteau

Page 83
1. false
2. false
3. true
4. true

Page 84
1. human-made chemicals
2. pests
3. bigger
4. Organic

Page 85
1. false
2. false
3. true
4. true

Page 86
1. a resting place for a person after he or she dies
2. a ruler of ancient Egypt
3. They believed it would let the pharaoh live forever.
4. the Great Pyramid of Giza

Page 87
1. false
2. false
3. false
4. true

Page 88
1. "Fat Tuesday"
2. eat a lot
3. French explorers
4. New Orleans, Louisiana

Page 89
1. b
2. b
3. a
4. c

Page 90
1. So their enemies don't know their plans.
2. the Japanese
3. the Navajo
4. Answers will vary but may include: There was no way to write their language. Navajo words are hard to say. Many words have many different meanings.

Page 91
long eyelashes—block blowing sand
wide feet—keep from sinking into sand
pads on knees—protect from hot sand
leathery mouths—protect from thorny plants
fatty humps—store energy

Page 92
1. baseball, basketball, football, and track
2. in 1945
3. baseball leagues for African American players
4. He was the first African American to play in the major leagues since the late 1800s.

Page 93
1. a ship called the *Mayflower*
2. Plymouth Colony
3. Squanto
4. harvest festival

Image Credits